T0194993

It is a joy and honor to pastor a church in a military community where many understand service over self. But it is also a challenge. We pray for our airmen and soldiers as they leave for dangerous deployments. We try to minister to the families they leave behind. But too often we fall short to adequately care for the needs of our military women, and our deployed servicemen's wives, due to a lack of understanding of the difficulties they face. Aurelia Smith has just made our job much easier! As a former military woman, spouse of an Air Force officer, and certified Biblical counselor, Aurelia has the Biblical acumen and personal experience to write this wonderful guide for offering help and hope to military women in a way that relevantly applies the balm of God's Word to the root heart issues. This book is sound, practical, and eminently helpful… I found myself devouring page after page, wishing that I had been able to read it years ago. I highly recommend *Ministering to Military Women* to pastors, counselors, chaplains, and laymen who would seek to understand and serve our brave military women (and military spouses) by properly applying the enduring power of God's Word.

Troy Hamilton
Pastor, Rocky Bayou Baptist Church, Niceville, FL

• •

There is no better guide for a person who needs hope and help than someone who has been through the same challenges and pitfalls, who is very wise in the authoritative scriptures and who can therefore give compassionate insights. Aurelia is that person, as she and her husband have not only served in the military for 27 years but have made it their life, a life where they have sought not only to sacrifice for their country, but to glorify God. In this book she addresses the pertinent information she ascertained through a sizeable survey of military women. Aurelia is balanced in sharing first-hand both the blessings of military life along with its challenges. She offers practical, robust counsel to those who want help through a growing personal relationship with Jesus Christ and the resources found in the ever- relevant Word of God. Smith's real-life approach sets this book apart in that she has thorough experience in the problems, and straight-forward biblical counsel to address them. As you read this book you will find wise counsel to equip you for victory in the most important battles that you will ever face—those of the soul..

Mary Somerville
Adjunct Professor, The Master's University

• •

Aurelia Smith's work provides a unique and insightful window into the important and selfless lives of women in the "military milieu." As a retired senior NCO, I can attest that the information in these pages will provide practitioners, scholars, policy advisors and those who minister and counsel military women an awakening of critical consciousness that will enhance their capacity to serve our military members and their families.

Dr. Edgar Dillard
SMSgt. USAF Ret.
Board Chairman Family Support Ciricle, Inc.

• •

Aurelia targets the women in military service and the wives of military service personnel. She challenges these strong women to incorporate biblical principles along with specific and accurate scriptures in their personal battles with such issues as fear, controlling attitudes, bitterness, and resentment. Aurelia offers biblical and theological solutions (with homework) to the unique and real needs of these women. She challenges local churches and Christian counselors to come along side the women who serve and support our military. Aurelia's research resonates with me as a wife of a retired Army Chaplain. She showcases a group of women who can be classified as "The silent strength of the military".

Delores Rice Brown, Ph.D and Alex Brown, D.Min
Chaplain, US Army Retired

• •

After over 20 years in the military, I've either experienced, or known other women who have experienced, each of the challenges that Aurelia describes with such clarity and insight. During my career, I've come alongside many active duty friends who were struggling and I only wish I'd been armed with Aurelia's concise analysis and discussion of biblical truths. For me personally, what a great reminder to rest in the joy of our Lord's constant truths-- while uprooting life every few years!"

Valarie A. Long

• •

The life of a military woman (active duty or spouse) contains many elements foreign to her civilian counterparts. Understanding these unique elements will help a counselor minister to these women with more compassion and clearer objectives as they bring Scripture to bear upon the desires, temptations, and struggles their counselees face. In addition to providing a window into the lives of military women, the Scriptures and homework assignments will be helpful resources for issues all women face.

Jennessa Randall
ACBC Certified Counselor; 18yr Cadence
International Missionary-ministering to active
duty women and wives, overseas and stateside

• •

Aurelia Smith is well qualified to speak into the lives of military families as her bio illustrates. Her qualifications derive not only from her personal military experience but from her love of God's Word and her reliance on the Word to inform and discipline her thoughts, motives and wisdom. All of the above is superseded by her love for people inspired by the love Jesus Christ has shown her. She and her husband, Nathan, devote their time and talents for the Glory of God in everything they do. Expect to be challenged in your thinking and spurred on to Glorify God in your own life.

Stacy Rech
ACBC Certified Counselor

• •

Aurelia Smith provides wise Biblical counseling from first-hand experience as a former active duty member and as a current military spouse. Her insight into the struggles common among women associated with the military community shows the depth of her understanding of these unique challenges. Aurelia's passion for seeing women overcome the issues they wrestle with is clearly evident throughout her book. By countering common approaches of seeking relief from struggles with methods that do not effectively address the root of the issue, Aurelia seeks to help women find lasting heart transformation. Her approach is solidly founded upon the life-changing hope of the Gospel, rests firmly on the life-giving power of Scripture and employs the life-sustaining ministry of the Holy Spirit. This book serves as a tremendous resource for those seeking to better understand the issues facing women in the military community and offers practical applications for those desiring to minister to them.

Megan Schuliger
Air Force spouse, former PWOC Spiritual
Life VP; Key Spouse mentor

• •

As a military chaplain who has deployed on numerous occasions, my wife has experienced firsthand many of the blessings and challenges addressed in this work. I have been waiting for a resource such as this to be written so that I can be a better husband to my wife and a better chaplain to the military women seeking counsel. Aurelia Smith has masterfully granted the reader key insights into what our women face in military life, as well as, given the reader the source of true help and hope that is available in God's written Word. I highly recommend this valuable resource to all who provide counsel and care for military women.

Major David S. Merrifield
Deputy Wing Chaplain
United States Air Force

• •

What an amazing resource for those who counsel, mentor, and disciple women in the military context! Timely, incisive, and delivered with first hand accuracy, Aurelia Smith exposes the multi-faceted and unique lifestyle, which must be understood before meaningful, scripture-grounded counsel can be delivered to a clearly underserved population of our military ranks. This work addresses the heart of military women (active and spouses) as key to biblical change and hope. This author champions the equipping of "iron to sharpen iron" in the call to equip and accredit an army of women of this singular community to minister to each other. After twenty-seven years of active duty and nearly twelve years of para-church ministry to the military community, we are heartened to see how this resource will engender transformation in women, families, the military, communities at large, and our nation. As women through counsel are helped to see the Author of life in their lives as sufficient, gracious, and enduring, the challenges of their complex, sometimes tempestuous, lives will be viewed rightly, and they will begin to flourish. *Ministering to Military Women* is a complete, strategic, and fresh offering in an area of virtually non-existent resources. Aurelia Smith deftly elevates every struggle of life to the perspective of God's sovereignty and goodness. Seen from this height, right thinking and right being will ensue.

Colonel (Air Force Ret) Larry and Bobbie Simpson
Officers' Christian Fellowship's Spiritually Smart
Families, Authors and Conference facilitators

• •

Ministering to Military Women:
Biblical Help & Hope

Aurelia M. Smith

WESTBOW
PRESS®
A DIVISION OF THOMAS NELSON
& ZONDERVAN

WestBow Press books may be ordered through booksellers or by contacting:

WestBow Press
A Division of Thomas Nelson & Zondervan
1663 Liberty Drive
Bloomington, IN 47403
www.westbowpress.com
1 (866) 928-1240

THE HOLY BIBLE, NEW INTERNATIONAL VERSION®,
NIV® Copyright © 1973, 1978, 1984, 2011 by Biblica, Inc.®
Used by permission. All rights reserved worldwide.

ISBN: 978-1-9736-3695-3 (sc)
ISBN: 978-1-9736-3697-7 (hc)
ISBN: 978-1-9736-3696-0 (e)

Library of Congress Control Number: 2018909740

Print information available on the last page.

WestBow Press rev. date: 8/17/2018

To Nate, my Knight in Shining Armor, who instead of riding in on a horse, piloted an F-16 "Viper" instead! I definitely prefer the fighter jet. You are a gift and I am so thankful for our marriage. I love you.

To my parents for their kindness, enthusiasm, sacrificial service to our family and great love. I thank God for you!

To my Redeemer and Lord for his amazing grace, life-altering love and faithfulness.

• •

Contents

Introduction

If you are a woman in uniform, I identify with you! My time in the military gave me a framework from which to understand some of what you face. If you are a woman married to a man in uniform, I desire to be of service to you and share what has encouraged me as the spouse of a military member. If you are someone ministering to these, my sisters, I long to give you an accurate and loving view into the context in which we as military women, hope, struggle, dream, grow, raise our families and bravely serve. It is my hope that as a result of reading this book, you will be better able to point the military women you counsel, encourage and come alongside, to the help and hope found in Christ and the Scriptures.

Many years ago I wrote several chapters of the beginning of this book under rather classic military circumstances. My husband was deployed to a dangerous location in the Middle East. I had two young sons who were in elementary school. I also struggled with some life-threatening health challenges that were at times incapacitating. Before my husband returned from his deployment, we learned that he was going to be re-assigned to a different base in a completely different state. This meant that our home where we were living (CA) needed to be rented or sold and that preparations needed to be made to transfer to a new state (OH), all while he was half-way around the world! By the end of that fateful year, I felt as if I had lived three distinct lives. My children also had to endure much. Not only did they miss their daddy for most of the year, but they said goodbye to friends, church family, and all that was familiar more than once. In fact, by the end of that year they had attended three different schools in three different states (CA, GA, OH). Not only adults serve. Our military children serve too and make countless sacrifices!

Oddly enough, lest you think my military adventures are over, as I work to get this manuscript printed into book form, I find myself in another somewhat classic military circumstance. Although my husband is not deployed, he's been away on several rather long temporary duty (TDY) assignments in various locations. Although my sons are older, they still miss their dad in this new season of their lives as they transform into young men. Even though I've experienced years of life in the military (my whole life to be honest!) as a child military dependent, military officer and active duty spouse, I still have very hard days in this challenging context (big girls do cry on occasion by the way...)! I know my military sisters can identify and that someone, somewhere, is probably shouting "AMEN!" No amount of experience in this context, even a lifetime, will make you or I immune to the various slings and arrows inherent in the military. We can never be strong enough or experienced and savvy enough to do it on our own! For victory, we must learn to rely on our Mighty Rock and King moment by moment.

So, although I can identify and sympathize with you, it is my desire to go beyond alerting those who counsel women like us to the very hard backdrop of military life in which we live. By God's grace, it is my hope that you will be drawn into a deeper walk with the Lord Jesus Christ. It is my prayer that you will view your military circumstances through the lens of Scripture and see the mighty hand of God at work in the most difficult of times. It is my aim to give you biblical help and hope! Not only for yourself, but for the many other women who are on this journey alongside of you.

Chapter 1

Why Focus on Military Women?
How Do I Use This Book?

This book sheds spiritual and biblical light on some of the lesser-known problems of the women who currently serve our nation-women veterans and women who are spouses to military members. There are five reasons for the importance and significance of this focus. First, years of war, deployment, and high operations tempo since 9/11 have made high demands of both military members and their families. Not only do active duty members serve, but so do their spouses and children. Second, female military members have contributed to our nation's defense in combat zones and operations, and their stories and involvement are little known. They, too, have challenges and problems upon their return to the United States that may look different than their male counterparts. Third, there is increasing interest in military members and their families from the White House, that funnels down to the rest of our society.[1] While it is good to mobilize different sectors of our nation's agencies to support military members and their families, the church of Jesus Christ has real answers to real problems with

---

[1] The White House, "Joining Forces: Taking Action to Serve America's Military Families," http://www.whitehouse.gov/joiningforces [accessed November 2011].

an indestructible hope to offer that no government initiative can even begin to administer. Fourth, an explosion of resources exists for the military member to use to address his or her problems. However, the perspective of the majority of these retreats, books, and counseling comes from a humanistic and psychological perspective, even within Christian circles. Fifth and finally, several studies and resource options exist for the male military member, but there is a sad lack of studies and resources for women who serve, whether they are active duty, reserve, guard, or a spouse.

In order to properly understand women and the unique military milieu and assist them in overcoming temptations and sins for God's glory, this book will be divided into three major parts. The first section will highlight both the blessings and challenges of life in the military so that the reader can better grasp the environment in which his or her counselees live, work, and raise their families. The second section of this book will include an analysis of methodology, as well as present data that includes firsthand interviews, on-line survey results of 114 participants, and information from various books, magazines, and audio sources pertinent to this topic. The third section will hone in on the top three temptations or sin areas as identified in the on-line survey created during the data-gathering phase for this book. Each temptation/sin will be presented in four parts. First, an example in the form of a case study in the military context will be shared. Second, the secular/psychological solutions to this problem will be highlighted. Third, the biblical and theological solutions to the problem will be presented. These solutions will include key passages from Scripture; how one's union with Christ, the Person of Christ, and the gospel impact this problem; and how one may need to change in thought, word, and deed by God's grace. Fourth, homework assignments and resources will be presented for each of the three problematic sin areas identified so that the biblical counselors will have a resource ready to use with their counselees.

There are four intended uses for this book. The first purpose is to familiarize the Church of Christ with the military milieu and some of the challenges women associated with this context face. Pastors, women's group leaders, or laymen with military members in their midst will be better able to shepherd, carry the burdens, and practice the "one-anothers"[2] of Scripture with their military-affiliated women if they have a better grasp of both the joys and hardships of this context. The second intended use of this book is to be a beginning resource for biblical counselors who counsel military-affiliated women. In order to build a truly helpful relationship, one must have some form of understanding regarding the context of the counselee. Furthermore, biblical counsel will be hindered if instruction and implementation are based on an inaccurate understanding of the military context. When a counselor knows some of the challenges, temptations, and sins that are connected to this unique operating environment, he or she is better enabled to provide counsel that is cogent, effective, and immediately applicable for God's glory. The third intended use of this book is to provide a ready resource to organizations that already minister to military women. Organizations such as the Association of Certified Biblical Counselors (ACBC),[3] Officers' Christian Fellowship (OCF), the Navigators, Cadence International, and the Chaplaincy may be blessed by a resource that not only identifies common sins and temptations of this group but that also targets the heart as the key to biblical change. The

---

[2] This refers to all the "one another" passages listed in the New Testament, for which believers are called to act in unity, love, forgiveness, encouragement, devotion, and service for Christ (Ephesians 4:32, John 13:34, Colossians 3:12, Romans 12:10, and 1 Thessalonians 5:11 are a few examples).

[3] ACBC has been certifying biblical counselors to ensure doctrinal integrity and to promote excellence in biblical counseling for forty years. Their website, biblicalcounseling.com is a wealth of information. You can find a certified biblical counselor at the site, tap into their many resources, like podcasts, to grow in your application of God's Word to everyday life, or learn about training and conferences being offered near you.

fourth intended use of this book is to come alongside Christian women affiliated with the military and offer a tool that enables them to view their lives and problems in a God-honoring way through the lens of Scripture. This book should remind them that they are not alone, there is help and hope in the gospel of Jesus Christ, God's Word is sufficient, and it is indeed possible to overcome sins and temptations by God's grace.

Chapter 2

The Blessings of Military Life

United States military life brings with it many positive benefits.[4] Health care, educational opportunities, stable employment, camaraderie, and provision of housing are just a few of the positives to which any secular-minded individual could point out.[5] However, this chapter will go beyond this in order to focus on some of the unique blessings bestowed on the child of God who is affiliated with the military. While there are numerous blessings associated with the military lifestyle, the following chapter will highlight six specific blessings in which women who serve in the military environment partake.

There is a twofold purpose in highlighting these blessings. First, a better understanding of these blessings can serve as an encouraging reminder to women who are going through trial in the military milieu. In the hardships of everyday life or in the cauldron of crisis, it is easy to lose sight of God's blessings. Remembering these will assist Christian women in the military

---

[4] Heidi Luedtke, "How the Science of Gratitude Can Change Your Military Life," *Military Spouse*, January 2012, 52. In this article, military spouses list eight things they are most appreciative of in the military.

[5] See the Secretary of Defense 1996 Annual Defense Report, Appendix G "Personnel Readiness Factors by Race and Gender" for a discussion of factors that influence youth to enlist in the military. http://www.dod.mil/execsec/adr96/appendix_g.html [accessed January 12, 2012].

milieu to "be joyful in hope, patient in affliction, faithful in prayer" and to "be joyful always; pray continually; give thanks in all circumstances" (Rom. 12:12; 1 Thess. 5:16-18). Second, a thorough understanding of just a few of the spiritual blessings associated with military life will help equip the church, biblical counselors, and para-church organizations that minister to military women. These can serve to better educate counselors who are unaware of the unique blessings of this way of life, and can also assist them in instilling hope in their counselees, a key component to the methodology of biblical counseling. Wayne Mack states the following about how biblical counselors can help others to think biblically about the opportunity for good in their situations and thus instill hope:

> Sometimes people lack hope because they see only the negative side of their circumstances and fail to recognize the potential for good that exists in every situation. They only see the problems and the pain; they do not see what God wants to accomplish through the situation. We need to help them realize that when God pushes us out of our comfort zone, He does so for the purpose of our growth and development.[6]

A Chance to Mirror Christ - Sacrificial Service

Women in the military milieu often are called upon to serve sacrificially, silently, and in seclusion. The woman in uniform gives of her time, talents, and even her own life if it is asked of her for a greater good. The spouse gives of her energy, time,

---

[6] John F. MacArthur and Wayne A. Mack, *Introduction to Biblical Counseling: A Basic Guide to the Principles and Practice of Counseling* (Dallas: Word Publishing, 1994), 203.

and talents to support her husband in whatever role he is called to fulfill, whether that be in a combat zone, amidst hazardous duties stateside, or through prolonged periods of separation and upheaval. Women in the military milieu are often called to serve as father and mother, teacher, disciplinarian, provider, nurse, domestic, cook, and caregiver all rolled into one.

Biblical counselors will want to remind the believer in Christ who serves sacrificially in this milieu to look to her Redeemer for wisdom, strength and grace. Jesus was the ultimate, sacrificing servant. He is the servant who was crushed and suffered for our iniquities (Isa. 53). He is the exalted One who willingly humbled Himself and took on the nature of a servant for our sake and for His Father's pleasure (Phil. 2:5-9). When women in the military milieu are overcome by the enormity of this sacrificial call to service and their seemingly relentless hard circumstances, they can be encouraged that they are actually blessed because they have been selected to mirror Christ to those around them. They can rest assured that Jesus, as their faithful High Priest, is interceding for them and will enable them to be faithful to this high calling for His name's sake (Heb. 2:17, 4:14-16, 7:25).

A Chance to Tangibly Participate in the Universal Church

While all believers are adopted into the universal church the moment they believe (Eph. 2:19; Col. 1:12), military women get to interact with other members of this extended family of faith in ways that many civilians never get the chance to experience this side of heaven. Frequent moves and relocations make it necessary to seek out a new church home at each duty station. The process of finding and identifying biblical churches across the United States and internationally is quite a challenge that can sometimes take months. However, when that search is complete, the woman in the military milieu has the privilege of seeing a whole new local body of believers at work. Whether stateside or abroad, she has the benefit of meeting, serving, and growing with brothers and sisters in Christ she might have otherwise never met if she stayed in one location. Julie Carlin, a retired Air Force spouse who is currently on staff with Navigators military ministry, shared the following about how God is using the military context for good in her life:

> I have ministered in the context of the military community my whole Christian walk so I have grown to love the people and the mission in a way I wouldn't have appreciated had I not been a military spouse. I have a greater appreciation for the cost of our freedom, both temporal and spiritual through Christ. Being affiliated with the military is one of the biggest blessings in my life.[7]

Counselors should remind the Christian woman in the military milieu that she gets to do much more than just see the world and experience its various cultures. As a child of God, she has the opportunity to meet God's people in every nation and place where she resides. This strategic placement gives her a better view of God's extravagant grace, His building up of the Church among all people, and a chance to savor communion and fellowship with the saints in a whole new light. Indeed, she has a sweet foretaste of what will come in the future when a new song will be sung to the Lamb about His blood, which purchased "men for God from every tribe and language and people and nation" (Rev. 5:9).

A Chance to Grow in God-Dependence

The United States as a nation places a high value on independence and self-sufficiency. Those who blaze their own trails and overcome seemingly insurmountable odds with true grit and self-determination

---

[7] Julie Carlin, interview by author, August 19, 2011.

are applauded, looked up to, and emulated by many. However, those who embrace the message of the cross recognize the truth that we can do nothing apart from Christ, and no one can boast about her own works in light of saving grace (John 15:5; Eph. 2:8-9). They are utterly dependent upon God for life, breath, provision, and salvation through His Son. Likewise, they also realize that they are interdependent with other believers for sanctification, growth, maturity, and fellowship (Eph. 4:11-16; Rom. 12:4-8).

Counselors can help a woman associated with the military to see the unique opportunity she has to experience the blessings of God-dependence on a large scale. A Christian woman in this milieu will recognize quickly that she absolutely cannot fulfill this calling on her own. Her reserves are not big enough. Her strength is not strong enough. Her intellect and planning powers are not sufficient to meet the challenges that are present or that lie ahead. Sara Horn, author and Navy Reserve spouse, describes in her book *God Strong*, the moment she understood her capabilities were not enough to see her through her husband's deployment:

> But sitting on the couch that day, worn out, spent, and ready to quit with no clear idea how I could do that, I came to another realization: that the strength I'd run on for so long was only my own and that already seven months into the deployment, I was missing what God was trying to teach me. That *my* strength had absolutely nothing to do with it.[8]

Just as all believers need to rely in faith and trust on Christ for salvation, women in the military milieu need to rely on Him daily in the face of solitary parenting, frequent moves, hazardous duties, and

---

[8] Sara Horn, *God Strong: The Military Wife's Spiritual Survival Guide* (Grand Rapids: Zondervan, 2010), 15.

navigating foreign terrain. Her distance from family and home-town friends will give her the opportunity to rely on God in ways that she might not have had before. The ever-present danger that surrounds life in the military, even during times of peace and routine training, will cause her to be more fervent in prayer and run to the shelter of her Father's wings (Psalm 17:8, 36:7, 91:4).[9] As she leans more fully in dependence on God in any and every situation she will have the delight of knowing His strength is sure, His wisdom is unfailing, His love is always operative, and His grace is sufficient.

A Chance to be Nontraditional Missionaries of the Gospel to the Nations

The woman in the military milieu often has golden opportunities to be a witness to the glories of Christ in realms where many others only dream. Wherever God in His sovereignty sends her for military duty, the believer can know that spiritual duty is of primary importance as well. Not only are women called to be good ambassadors of the United States on foreign soil, they are also called to be Christ's ambassadors, appealing and imploring those they meet in love to be reconciled to God (2 Cor. 5:20, Matt. 28:18-20). Women who are active duty, guard, reserve, or wives of military members are routinely sent overseas. There are also many opportunities for U.S. members and their families to meet individuals from foreign nations (coalition or allied forces) during stateside duties.

---

[9] Both in peace and in war, military service can be a dangerous profession. Casualties and wounded in action statistics inflicted in hostile environments like Iraq and Afghanistan are well known (see on-line published documents by Defense Manpower Data Center Data, Analysis and Programs Division that lists the Global War on Terrorism Casualty by Reason, 7 Oct, 2001 through 5 Dec, 2011). However, the day-to-day performance of routine training, proficiency and testing duties like flying, munitions, special forces, demolition duty, flight deck duty and parachute duty (just to name a few) incur numerous losses even during peacetime scenarios each year.

For the believer, each of these assignments is a chance for the gospel of Christ to be shared with new friends, new neighbors, new coworkers, and with foreign nationals who may never have heard the good news of salvation through Jesus Christ. Just as Esther was reminded by her cousin Mordecai, "And who knows but that you have come to royal position for such a time as this?" (Esther 4:14) Christian military women must remember that God lovingly selected them to be His representatives in a specific location, to specific people, and at a specific time for His purposes. She can rest assured that she is in a location, not because of a military personnel center jockeying assignments, but because God Himself sent her there on a mission for her good, the good of others she has yet to meet, and for His glory.

A Chance to Live Out Spiritual Realities - Authority, Submission, Roles and Responsibilities

Words like authority, submission, and gender roles are out of vogue today. The American culture in which we live increasingly rails against those in positions of authority. Furthermore, the very thought of submission, whether in the home, school or workplace, sets many people's teeth on edge and is viewed as irrational subservience. The cry and push for equality in all areas of life leaves many confused about who they are and what they should be doing in any given context.

Some civilians and secular mental health professionals may see the U.S. military's hierarchical and authoritarian stance as negative, especially in the midst of an increasingly egalitarian society.[10] However, the woman associated with the military milieu can be blessed with a clearer insight into the interaction of the Godhead, as well as an understanding of how her roles at home

---

[10] Lynn K. Hall, *Counseling Military Families: What Mental Health Professionals Need to Know* (New York: Routledge, 2008), 46, 118-119.

and in the church should be carried out if she has eyes to see. For instance, in the military there is a chain of command. Chain of command can be defined as, "The succession of commanding officers from a superior to a subordinate through which command is exercised."[11] Hence, those in authority hand down critical information and directives to their subordinates. Likewise, subordinates push concerns, ideas, and information up their chain of command. Innate to this structure are the ideas of submission, roles, and responsibilities at each level. This chain of command exists to maintain order and to insure that the right people are engaged with applicable information at any given time.

This is also the case spiritually for the believer. The Scriptures state that Christ is the Head of the Church and that believers are part of His Body (Col. 1:18; Eph. 1:22-23). Believers are called to obey and carry out the orders of their Lord and Master as expressed in Scripture (John 14:15; 1 John 2:3; 5:3). Even within the local body of believers, this spiritual chain of command exists since members are called to submit themselves to biblical leaders of the church (Heb. 13:17; 1 Thess. 5:12).

In the military, the rank structure from the highest ranking Flag officer to the newest and least-experienced Airman Basic, Private, or Seaman Recruit serves a purpose. Military law and custom requires those of lesser rank to show courtesy and deference to those of higher rank.[12] Obedience to military commands and

---

[11] Joint Education and Doctrine Division, J-7, Joint Staff, "DOD Dictionary of Military Terms," http://www.dtic.mil/doctrine/dod_dictionary/data/c/3019.html [accessed December 2011].

[12] The Uniform Code of Military Justice (UCMJ) addresses such issues as contempt for officials, disrespect toward superior commissioned officers, assault and willful disobedience, insubordinate conduct and failure to obey orders or regulations (articles 88-92). All articles of the UCMJ can be accessed on-line at "Uniform Code of Military Justice, Congressional Code of Military Law Applicable to all Military Members Worldwide," http://www.au.af.mil/au/awc/awcgate/ucmj.htm [accessed January 2012].

respect to military leaders are not given because those of higher rank are smarter, faster, better, or made of different stuff than the lesser in rank. The rank structure is in place to maintain order, aid command and control efforts, and so that missions can be accomplished effectively.

While comparisons between the Trinity and earthly authority are not exact, we do see facets of these same ideas about roles and submission at work in the Godhead also played out in the military context. Jesus was no less God because He submitted His will in perfect obedience to that of the Father (John 1:1; 4:34, 8:29, Phil. 2:5-11). The Holy Spirit also testifies to the beauty, truth, and atoning work of the Deity of Christ (John 14:26, 15:26). Each Person of the Godhead is no less God just because He has a different role, nor is He less than the others because He willingly submits to the authority of the other.

Likewise, Christian women are called to willingly place themselves under governing authorities (Rom. 13:1-2), the leadership of the church (Heb. 13:7), and to their husbands as unto the Lord (Eph. 5:22; Col. 3:18, Titus 2:5). Once again, this willing submission is not given because those in authority are smarter, stronger, faster, or better than she. Willing submission is done out of reverence for God. Voluntary submission is done with a desire for the gospel to go forth unhindered. Titus 2:5 states, "... so that no one will malign the word of God." Titus 2:8 states, "... so that those who oppose you may be ashamed because they have nothing bad to say about us." Titus 2:10 states, "...so that in every way they will make the teaching about God our Savior attractive." These various "so that" statements tell us how pivotal a believer's submission, self-control, and respect are to the message of the gospel. When a woman willingly submits to those over her, God's word is honored rather than maligned. Finally, this intentional submission is done with an understanding that all authority is established by God Himself (Rom. 13:1-7).

Aurelia M. Smith

A Chance to Orient Life Heavenward - This is not My Home

It is not unusual for military members and their families to relocate and transition to new duty locations every one to three years. If deployments or long-term temporary duties are also a part of a given assignment, the military spouse's family could relocate even more if they seek to garner support from out-of-state (or out of country) family members while their military member is gone. Each of these moves requires not only a change of address, but a complete life transition in the realms of church, schools, work, friends, and community.

At first glance, this may not seem like much of a blessing. Precious friends are left behind. Children are uprooted from their schools and neighborhoods. Churches say good-bye to members in whom they have invested, loved, and served sacrificially. Military members and their families have to begin once more in new locations without their prior support networks. However, there is much to this facet of the military milieu that a woman can embrace if she is willing and aware. Just as Abram in Genesis 12:1 was called to "leave your country, your people and your father's household," military women are called to do the same in faith and trust in God's sovereignty, provision, and love. Believers are reminded again and again in the pages of Scripture that life is temporal. Our short earthly existence is likened to grass (Psalm 103:15-16; 1 Pet. 1:24), fleeting shadows (Job 14:2; Psalm 144:4; 1 Chron 29:15), mist or vapor (James 4:14) and a breath (Psalm 39:5, 144:4; Job 7:7). At the same time, the Bible speaks clearly about what the mind-set of the believer should be while she lives this temporal life. She is called to set her mind on things above and remember that her life is hidden in Christ (Col. 3:1-4), that her citizenship is in heaven (Phil. 3:20), and to look forward to a home of righteousness (2 Pet. 3:13). C.S. Lewis wrote, "I must keep alive in myself the desire for my true country, which I shall not find till after death; I must never let it get snowed under or turned aside; I must make it the main object of life to press on to that other country and to help others to do the same."[13]

In light of these scriptural truths, counselors can help the woman in the military use her short time on earth wisely for the glory of God. Like the faithful listed in Hebrews 11, she can admit with them that she is an "alien and stranger on earth" (Heb. 11:13). Each move and PCS can serve as a visible and tangible reminder to the woman of God in this milieu that this present duty assignment is not her home. The constant change can also keep her from giving in to the temptation to live as though this earth (along with all its trappings) is her permanent residence. Her real home is in heaven with her Redeemer and Lord. In his book entitled *Heaven*, Randy Alcorn invites all believers to anticipate the magnificent adventure to come:

> If you know Jesus, I'll be with you in that resurrected world. With the Lord we love and with the friends we cherish, we'll embark together on the ultimate adventure in a spectacular new universe awaiting our exploration and dominion. Jesus will be the center of all things, and joy will be the air we breathe. And right when we think, "it doesn't get any better than this"- *it will.*[14]

Once there, farewells will be a thing of the past and tearful goodbyes will cease to exist.

---

[13] C.S. Lewis, *Mere Christianity* (New York: Simon and Schuster, 1952).

[14] Randy Alcorn, *Heaven* (Carol Stream, Illinois: Tyndale House Publishers, 2004), 457.

Chapter 3

The Challenges of Military Life

The military milieu is not an easy context in which to work, raise a family, or foster relationships. In the forward of a book written for secular mental health professionals,[15] Mary Wertsch summed up the stressful military context this way:

> Even in peacetime, such families must cope with the extraordinary pressures of a very stringent and demanding way of life:...with its lack of autonomy and limited privacy, financial stress, tours of duty that take father, mother, or both away from the family for long periods, frequent uprootings, and the ever-present possibility of injury or death. In addition, the youthfulness of service members, most of whom are married, means they may lack the wisdom and maturity to sort out the difficult problems they face-and this is only exacerbated by the extreme mobility of military life, which cuts

---

[15] Although this quote is from a psychologized and secular individual, her observation and comments are appropriate. However, despite the aptness of her summation as to the stressors of military life, believers who have been given every spiritual gift (Eph 1:3), who trust in the sufficiency of Scripture and who are united as part of the Bride of Christ will come to vastly different conclusions as to the methodology and solutions to these challenges and problems.

them off from the emotional sustenance of relatives
and friends that might otherwise see them through.
If someone were asked to design an environment
that would be as tough as possible on family systems,
it would probably look a lot like the military.[16]

There are innumerable challenges inherent to the military way
of life, but the following chapter will highlight six select challenges
that women who serve in the military environment face. There
are three reasons for highlighting these challenges. First, biblical
counselors, churches, and organizations that minister to women
in the military milieu will be better equipped to serve if they
have a greater understanding of the common challenges associated
with this lifestyle. Key components of the methodology of biblical
counseling, like compassionate involvement, a capability to rightly
interpret counselee data, instruction, and effective implementation
all rest on truly striving to know the environment and context
of the military individual. Wayne Mack states the following in
regard to developing a helping relationship with any counselee:

In counseling, as in any other relationship, we
must remember that *our impact and influence in
people's lives is usually related to their perception
of us.* That is why involvement is so important to
the counseling process. Usually, the counseling
process is truly effective only when an acceptable
level of involvement has been established...The
facilitative relationship must be built on the
foundations of *compassion, respect,* and *sincerity.*[17]

---

[16] Lynn K. Hall, *Counseling Military Families: What Mental Health
Professionals Need to Know* (New York: Routledge, 2008), X.

[17] John F. MacArthur and Wayne Mack, *Introduction to Biblical Counseling:
A Basic Guide to the Principles and Practice of Biblical Counseling* (Dallas:
Word Publishing, 1994), 175.

Second, those who are already experienced members of the military milieu may be encouraged to see that some of the areas in which they have silently struggled over the years are indeed common in this lifestyle and that they are not alone. Third, women who are new to the military milieu may read this chapter in order to mentally and spiritually prepare themselves for what may lie ahead on their journey, trusting that God will provide grace for each of these challenges when they arise. This chapter will not attempt to answer or give solutions to every one of these challenges, but will simply seek to inform. Later chapters will meet specific sins and temptations that arise in the context of these challenges head on with the Person of Jesus Christ, the all-sufficient Word of God, and the riches found within the community and household of God so that the redeemed woman in the military milieu can overcome by His grace.

The Search and Discovery of a Biblical Local Church Challenge

The Scriptures teach that when a woman is reconciled with Christ, she is automatically placed in a new relationship with other members of the redeemed. Union with Christ brings communion with all for whom Christ died. She is now a member of God's household, with brothers and sisters in the faith (Eph. 2:19). She is now qualified to share in the inheritance of the saints (Col. 1:12; Eph. 1:18). "Believers compose one priesthood, one nation, one race, one temple, one plant, one flock, one family, and one body. We have all been made one spiritually, and we belong together in communion, living out that oneness in local churches."[18] As such, through this communion of believers comes many answers to the challenges that will be discussed. Members of the local body are called to minister both physically and spiritually to women

---

[18] Wayne A. Mack and David Swavely, *Life in the Father's House: A Member's Guide to the Local Church* (Phillipsburg: P&R Publishing, 1996), viii.

in the military milieu with their God-given gifts. These sisters and brothers in Christ become a new family and a home away from home for the military member and her family. However, the process of identifying, finding, and becoming a contributing member of biblical churches across the United States and internationally is no easy feat that the counselor must be aware of![19] Even if a military member knows what the hallmarks are of a biblical local church, the search and membership process could take months.

This challenge is even further compounded by what may be available at any given duty station. The woman serving at an unknown duty location in Pakistan or Afghanistan has a severely-limited choice as to corporate worship arenas. The woman serving in the Marines or Navy may be ship bound and have very little choice as to corporate worship for months at a time. The American family stationed in Europe, South America, Asia, or Africa also has many challenges to overcome in the realms of language, location (how far the church is from where they are stationed), doctrine, and practice. Finally, even when a military installation offers denominational services at home or abroad, the Protestant umbrella is very wide. The military Protestant banner can include anything from Baptist, Episcopalian, and Seventh Day Adventist to Latter-Day Saints (Mormon) chaplains.[20] This means that the various liturgical, evangelical, or gospel services offered under the Protestant community may not be in line with what the military member believes is true about the public proclamation of the

---

[19] Part of the problem may be that some in the military milieu may not even know what the distinguishing characteristics of a biblical church are. It is here that the biblical counselor can help the counselee see what the church is, how it is to function and the counselee's role in it according to the Scriptures.

[20] A discussion of what mainline denominations are included under the military Protestant category was obtained via phone conversation. Air Force Chaplain, personal communication, Wright Patterson AFB, OH, December 29 2011.

Word, the sufficiency of the Scriptures, the doctrines of grace, church leadership, and ecclesiology, to name a few.

The Marriage Strain Challenge

Biblical counselors and those seeking to help women in the military milieu should be aware that there are several factors that can serve to strain a marital bond. Divorce and infidelity are all too common among military marriages (future chapters will discuss the temptations toward emotional and physical infidelity that a military woman faces). When one considers recent data showing that military women are almost seven times more likely to be married to another service member (dual military marriage) than are their male counterparts,[21] it is obvious that the strains on a marriage can reach epidemic proportions. The pace of military life, even in the absence of war, can strain marital ties. Some military platforms and those who operate them are always in high demand in almost every area of operation, even during peacetime. For example, crews that operate Intelligence, Surveillance and Reconnaissance aircraft like the RC-135 Rivet Joint and personnel who are members of the military police or security forces are always in high demand. This high operations tempo requires military members to be absent for long intervals from their families and spouses. If both members of the marriage are not tenacious about identifying and solving their problems biblically, this factor will only compound them. After all, it is difficult, or next to impossible to resolve a problem if one member of the marriage is hardly ever present. Marshele Carter Waddell, a Navy SEAL wife, puts it this way: "A service member's time away from home for training and for deployment adds stresses that wives of civilians do not encounter with the same intensity.

---

[21] Andrew Tilghman, "Gender Gap Shows in Demographics, Opinions," *Air Force Times*, January 2, 2012.

The top temptation is to give up on the marriage and to take an easier path. A military marriage comes with all the responsibilities of legal/spiritual union, but very little of the joy of companionship and intimacy."[22]

Frequent moves from duty station to duty station can be a source of marital strain. The time in anticipation of a new move, during the move, and directly after a move can be incredibly stressful. A myriad of choices have to be made, like "Where will we live?" (This depends on the duty station; on-base housing is not an option due to a lack of availability.) "What do we need to get rid of to lighten our load for when the movers arrive?" "What can our budget afford during this moving and initial set up process?" (Military pay often falls short of all that needs to be accomplished during a move and whatever reimbursement that does occur happens mostly *after* the move is complete. The problem is further compounded when a military family owns homes in other states.)[23] "Where will the children go to school?" (The question goes beyond homeschooling, private schooling or public schooling. This question also considers if the children are at a time in their education in which this move will hamper their graduation or eligibility for certain programs.) Details from interstate compacts on education, and car registration, all the way to how a family wants to set up the placement of their furniture can put added stress and tension on raw, weary, nerves.

Should a military spouse be actively engaged in furthering her education, or if she is employed outside of the home, each subsequent move will mean even more upheaval. Will credits

---

[22] Marshele Waddell, interview by author, August 28, 2011.

[23] A Permanent Change of Station (PCS) survey conducted by the National Military Family Association revealed that "more than 50% of the respondents identified uncovered expenses related to the move as one of the top three moving challenges." National Military Family Association, *"PCS Survey Executive Summary For Moves Between 2008-2010,"* http://www.militaryfamily.org/publications/survey-reports-guides/ [accessed January 2012].

transfer? Will previous courses at another academic institution be accepted at the new location? Will this move mean lower pay and/or a lesser position at her new civilian workplace? Is her skill set even represented in the vicinity of this new duty location, or will she have to travel extreme distances to practice it? In the face of these stressors and questions, some wives decide to not move to the next duty location along with their spouses. Choosing to live apart can often exacerbate weak spots in struggling marriages.

Circumstantially-induced single-parenting that occurs as part of the military milieu can be extremely difficult on a marriage. Mothers who are left behind during prolonged separation are required to take over in ways they perhaps never imagined. Many wives not only care for the children and all of their needs, but sometimes they even give birth to subsequent children without their spouses present. (Articles below discuss the "flat-daddy" revolution and how these life-size pictures are showing up everywhere, including the birthing and delivery room.)[24] Even when a military husband is not deployed, long duty hours and frequent mandatory travel make it very difficult to be involved to the extent that their wives desire. Because of this, cooking, cleaning, instructing, correcting, disciplining, nurturing, and even fathering falls on the wife's shoulders during a father's absence. When a husband and father does return, he may find it difficult to enter back into his place as leader, simply because his wife has had to make scores of decisions in his place in regard to the children, their schedules, and their home. Sometimes, resentment exists in the heart of the wife because she lacks the help and support she needs from her husband in raising the children because of the long hours, temporary assignments, and deployments.

Finally, hindrances to communication can be difficult

---

[24] Jon R. Anderson, "Flat Daddies Keep Memories Alive for Fallen Soldier's Family," and "Life Size Cutouts Are Keeping Families Connected," *Air Force Times*, April 28 2011.

on a military marriage. Despite the prolific nature of mobile technology, military couples are often unable to communicate in vital ways based on their context. For instance, while e-mail is often an option, it too may be intermittent in some locations (i.e., aboard a military ship). Furthermore, some subjects are very difficult to address via e-mail (that is being monitored, no less). Software applications like Skype or Facetime do offer some connectivity to troops and their families, but in some locations these links are highly variable. Imagine the chagrin a woman feels when she is tearfully explaining her problems and prayer concerns to her husband several time zones away, and her session is suddenly lost. In some cases, several days may go by before she hears from her loved one again. Alysia Patterson Mueller shares in her article entitled iHusband:

> When your husband is deployed, losing your phone is more than an inconvenience-it's downright scary. You're instantly filled with the fear that you might miss one of his few and precious phone calls. And then, the stomach-sinking feeling when you find the phone and see 'Missed Call,' knowing there's no way to call back and he might not have another chance to call you for days.[25]

Some military members are unable to use the phone, e-mail, send a letter, or use any other form of communication for long stretches due to the covert nature of their mission. In these cases, their loved ones do not hear from them until they return, the mission is complete, or they are authorized to open lines of communication again. These kinds of interruptions and hindrances in communication can severely challenge a couple as

---

[25] Alysia Patterson Mueller, "iHusband," *Military Spouse*, February 2012, 36.

they try to work through heart issues or address problems in their marriage or their family.

The effects of these challenges are well documented by several surveys, articles, and studies. Military marriages are at high risk. Recent data from the Pentagon shows that "military women also are far more likely to get divorced. In fiscal 2011, 8 percent of married women got a divorce, compared with 3 percent of married military men."[26] According to a study entitled "Comparing Rates of Marriage and Divorce in Civilian, Military, and Veteran Populations" after leaving military service, veterans have a higher divorce rate than their civilian counterparts.[27]

The Absence of Extended Family Challenge

Service in the United States military can take its members far and wide. According to September 30, 2011 data from the Department of Defense, there are 1,219,995 service members in the United States and its territories, 80,718 military personnel in Europe, 160 in the Former Soviet Union, 55,671 in East Asia and the Pacific, 6,270 service members in North Africa, Near East and South Asia, 654 military personnel in Sub-Saharan Africa, and 1,965 in the Western Hemisphere. There are over 100,000 Navy and Marine Corps members afloat and over 130,000 military members deployed in support of Operation Enduring Freedom in and around Afghanistan and other locations.[28]

---

[26] Andrew Tilghman, "Gender Gap Shows in Demographics, Opinions," *Air Force Times*, January 2, 2012.

[27] Benjamin Karney, David Loughran and Michael Pollard, *"Comparing Rates of Marriage and Divorce in Civilian, Military, and Veteran Populations,"* http://www.paa2008.princeton.edu/abstractViewer.aspx?submissionid=81696 [accessed January 2012].

[28] Department of Defense Military Personnel Statistics, *"Active Duty Military Personnel Strengths by Regional Area and By Country (309A) September 30, 2011,"* http://sladapp.dmdc.osd.mil/personnel/MILITARY/miltop.htm [accessed January 17, 2012].

With these types of numbers at duty locations both stateside and overseas, there is a good chance that women associated with the military milieu will be moving far from their childhood homes and support networks. When this happens, the support that she used to derive from her extended family may no longer be available due to distance and expense. Parents are no longer around the corner in times of crisis. Grandparents, aunts, uncles, cousins, and other supportive family members are no longer within the easy reach of a car trip.

While technology does help in some instances to communicate with those she loves, in person interaction at birthdays, weddings, new births, reunions, or even just everyday events of life can not be replaced. Who will care for her children while she is deployed? Where can the spouse turn for help while she struggles with debilitating health issues on a daily basis while her husband serves? Who will offer a loving and helping hand in the midst of setting up a new home in a new community with new responsibilities where she knows no one? Who will come alongside the spouse left behind as she faces an empty chair and setting at her table and a vacant spot next to her as she tries to sleep night after night?[29]

The Anonymity and Isolation Challenge

If women associated with the military milieu do not fight against the challenging effects of anonymity and isolation, the gypsy lifestyle of the military context can lend itself to serious implications and consequences. A move across the country into a new community lends itself to isolation simply because until military members and their families begin to make contacts, they may be seen but not known. A move to an overseas location where

---

[29] Once again, as a believer, the short answer to this string of questions is her family in Christ. Her union with Christ and communion with other believers in the faith form a new unit of support no matter where she is on the globe.

language and cultural differences have to be learned and overcome can lead to further isolation.

Even when Christian military members seek out fellowship and involvement in a new local church, for a season they are for all intents and purposes anonymous. It takes time to become deeply involved in a church and to build relationships (time is something that military members and their families may find in short supply, especially if an assignment to a particular location is short). The leadership and members of the church may recognize a new face and her military occupation, but unless she chooses to open herself up, she will not truly be known by this new membership. Her past, her struggles, her strengths and weaknesses are unknown by those at her new location. In fact, because of a lack of accountability, if a woman has ungodly patterns of living, or is running from problems, this aspect of military life can hinder her from receiving the real help she needs.

Other times, isolation naturally occurs due to a husband's deployment, frequent temporary assignments that take him away from his family, or by a demanding duty schedule. In these circumstances, the mother with young children is often unable to participate with regularity in women's Bible studies or evening gatherings, which further isolates her from knowing others and being known. Likewise, if a woman is in active duty or serving in the military herself, she has fewer opportunities to bond with other women in Christian settings since she is typically working when many gatherings take place.[30]

Finally, anonymity and isolation sometimes occur by the choice of the military members or by the choice of their new community. Military women can be anonymous and isolated from the helping communities around them because they are seeking to guard their

---

[30] Parachurch organizations like Protestant Women of the Chapel can be a helpful way to link up with other military sisters in Christ, but they typically target wives of military husbands rather than the active duty female or the single military mother.

hearts from the pain that will occur when they move on to their next assignment. No matter how much experience a woman has with transitions, saying goodbye to those she loves leaves lasting pain. Jocelyn Green, author of *Faith Deployed* and former Coast Guard spouse, shared about an initial decision she made in an attempt to avoid the future pain of saying goodbye: "I had only been a military wife for a few months before I made a conscious decision to not get attached to people in our new town of Homer, Alaska. Still reeling from the good-byes from our previous home of Washington, D.C., I was trying to safeguard myself against the pain that would inevitably come when it was time to move on again."[31]

Likewise, local organizations and churches may be reticent to truly welcome military-affiliated women and their families into the fold because they are aware that their presence is only temporary. Instead of making full use of the friendships, gifts, and talents that God brings for a temporal season, they may hold the woman associated with the military milieu at arms length. Cathie Marcolesco, a retired Air Force spouse, encouraged churches to minister to military spouses in the following way: "Welcome them in the same way you would welcome someone 'permanent.' Sometimes a church family will...treat military (members) as temporary. It may not be just the church family, but also the military member contributing to the problem. As hard as it is, we all need to be willing to invest in the relationships, no matter how short."[32]

The Changed and Wounded Warrior Challenge

Sometimes, military members pay the ultimate, sacrificial price by laying down their lives while carrying out their duties stateside

---

[31] Jocelyn Green, *Faith Deployed: Daily Encouragement for Military Wives* (Chicago: Moody Publishers, 2009), 97. The rest of the story relates for the reader how Jocelyn embraced loving even though it would hurt in the future.

[32] Cathie Marcolesco, interview by author, June 21, 2011.

or abroad. Other times, our military members physically return from their deployments or missions, but they are not unscathed. Perhaps the military member lost compatriots or had to harm another human being in the course of duty and is struggling spiritually with the heavy grief and pain of these losses. Perhaps she was wounded in action and sustained injuries that leave her paralyzed or without the use of some of her limbs.[33] Perhaps her injuries are not outwardly visible, but are none-the-less real, such as in the case of Traumatic Brain Injury (TBI). The damage done to her brain can lead to "...permanent or temporary impairment of cognitive, physical, and psychosocial functions, with an associated diminished or altered state of consciousness."[34] Perhaps she was exposed to toxic elements in the air or water while she conducted her duties that are now wreaking havoc on her immune system and internal organs. Whatever the injury, when the member does return home, she is altered in various ways, sometimes permanently. A wife can come to the frightening realization that the soldier, airman, or sailor who returned is not the same man who left. In her book entitled *Faith Deployed: Daily Encouragement for Military Wives*, Jocelyn Green shared the following about a National Guard wife: "The hardest part of war wasn't her husband's deployment; it was when he first came home. His multiple concussions and his exposure to constant combat and chlorine gas resulted in loss of short-term memory and an extremely heightened sense of anxiety, which in turn resulted in frustration and anger."[35]

---

[33] Read more about female wounded veterans in this article by, Kelly Wallace, *"Female Wounded Warriors Thrive Together,"* http://www.cbsnews.com/8301-500803_162-4195938-500803.html [accessed January 17, 2012].

[34] Segun T. Dawodu, "Traumatic Brain Injury (TBI)-Definition, Epidemiology, Pathophysiology," http://www.emedicine.medscape.com/article/326510-overview [accessed January 2012].

[35] Jocelyn Green, *Faith Deployed: Daily Encouragement for Military Wives* (Chicago: Moody Publishers, 2009), 201.

The family members who now care for, encourage, and provide for the military member's needs will experience several battles. Family members not only assist the military member or veteran to get access to appropriate medical care, but they also seek to love their military members in the midst of trying to embrace a whole new life that they would not choose of their own accord. The demands and care giving needs that come with this challenge can have far-reaching impacts on the military member, the spouse, and the family. "The aftermath of war is a battle fought on the home front. Spouses and families who love and live with these vets day in and day out are fighting from unfamiliar foxholes against an enemy no one prepared them to face."[36]

The Ever-Present Danger Challenge

All life is fragile, and all believers should live as though the present day may be their last. However, counselors should be aware that on a daily basis, women that serve in the military milieu are reminded of the brevity of life and are acquainted with danger in ways that many civilians do not experience. Military service can be intensely dangerous, even for those career fields that are not traditionally thought of as "front line."

For instance, in hostile duty areas like Afghanistan, support troops from finance, medical, contracting, and logistics may find themselves just as much in harm's way as operators do. Lt. Zoe Bedell, who served as the Marine Female Engagement Team Officer-In-Charge in Afghanistan from October 2010 to April 2011, in her interview with PRI's *The World*, stated the following about the front line, "...there is no such thing as a front line in Afghanistan and the counter insurgency; and really any time

---

[36] Rev. Christopher B. Adsit, and Marshele Carter Waddell, *When War Comes Home: Christ-Centered Healing for Wives of Combat Veterans* (Newport News: Military Ministry Press, 2008), 7.

anyone leaves the wire, they're on the front line...that term doesn't necessarily apply as well anymore."[37] Even when our troops are at home and not in hostile areas, normal training, test missions and duties carry with them palpable risk factors. Some Air Force Specialty Codes (AFSC), Military Occupation Specialties (MOS) and Ratings have higher risks associated with their functions and are awarded Hazardous Duty Incentive Pay for a reason. For instance, Air Force pilots must maintain up to date papers on file that outline in detail how clergy and commanders should proceed to notify family members should an aircraft accident or loss occur. When a spouse hears via radio, internet, or television that an installation jet had an accident and that an unnamed aircrew member was injured or killed, each ring of the phone and each knock on the door can be an agonizing experience.

> When our nation decides to wage war, we women and men who love America's war-fighters comfort them when they call home sounding hollow; we manage their lives while they're gone - we pay their bills, service their cars, care for their children. We're told: "If there's a problem, don't cry to your spouses; there's nothing they can do about it, it will only distract them, and where they are, distractions can be fatal." So, we solve the problems ourselves. And while we're doing all that, we're waking up every morning knowing today could be the day the staff car pulls up in front of our house and two or three people in dress uniforms walk up to our door. Today could be the

---

[37] Lt. Zoe Bedell, interview by Marco Werman, PRI's *The World*, *"Female Marine Officer-In-Charge,"* http://www.theworld.org/2011/05/female-marine-officer-in-charg/ [accessed January 2012].

day our life as we know it disappears into a black hole of grief.[38]

Living in this type of constant danger environment can breed an ungodly fear for those women who do not take their thoughts to task and trust in the loving and all-wise sovereignty of God.

---

[38] Kristin Henderson, *While They're at War: The True Story of American Families on the Homefront* (Boston: Houghton Mifflin Company, 2006), 5.

Chapter 4

The Interviews: Temptations, Context and How the Local Church and Counselors Can Help

The first part of this book sought to arm the reader with an entry-level grasp of the environment in which military members live, work, and raise their families so as to assist them in compassionate involvement and instilling hope in their counselees. The purpose of this second part of the book is to equip churches, counselors, and organizations that minister to women in the military milieu with pertinent data that will provide them a backdrop in the data gathering process. In order to truly know a woman in the military milieu and to counsel effectively, it is essential to ask the right kind of questions. Paul Tripp, in explaining the importance of the second aspect, "know" in a personal relationship ministry, stated,

> ...you cannot know me only by knowing what Scripture says about me. You will know wonderfully helpful things about me as a human being, but you will not know how these truths are uniquely manifested in my life *without asking.* We must seek to know one another in a way that recognizes God both as our Creator (universal human truths) and as our sovereign Lord (the unique, individual details). This will not only

> make us thankful that we come armed with the truths of Scripture, but it will also drive us to know well the particular person God has sent our way.[39]

As such, the data collected and presented here can serve as a starting place from which to ask informed questions of the woman in the military milieu. The firsthand interviews, on-line survey results, and information from various other sources relevant to the topic will assist the reader in her own quest to better understand the unique individual and her context.

Method of Analysis

Data collection for the production of this book included three main forms. The first form of data collection came from readily available sources at various libraries, on-line materials, audio materials and programs, and published works on the subject. The information gleaned from these materials is interspersed throughout the book and provide necessary background data, and also serves as a secular, counter perspective to the biblical mode of thought and practice in some instances.

The second form of data collection came from firsthand interviews. These seven interviews were conducted in both traditional and nontraditional formats. Some interviews were conducted in the more conventional face to face design. Other interviews were collected in a more nontraditional setup in which the interviewer created questions in a document and sent the questions to the interviewee via electronic means. The interviewee then answered the questions on the same document and returned

---

[39] Paul David Tripp, *Instruments In the Redeemer's Hands: People In Need of Change Helping People In Need of Change* (Phillipsburg: P&R Publishing, 2002), 169-170.

the completed interview to the interviewer. Interviewees came from a varied representation of the Christian military community and included both retired and active duty spouses, a member of the military chaplaincy, full-time ministry workers with Cadence International and the military arm of Navigators, and three Christian published authors of nonfiction works designed to equip and encourage military women. Information gleaned from these interviews will be presented in this chapter.

The third form of data collection was an on-line survey created specifically for the purpose of providing relevant input from a wider Christian female military-affiliated audience for this book. The survey entitled, "Christian Women and the Military Top 5 Temptations" had eight questions designed to collect demographic data, military affiliation, what the respondents viewed as their top five temptations in the military milieu and from whom they sought help in overcoming these temptations. One hundred fourteen women took the survey and provided feedback between the dates of 9 June, 2011 and 16 October, 2011. Data from the on-line survey will be presented in the next chapter.

Presentation of Data From Interviews

Interviewees were representative of all of the services except the Marines (Air Force, Navy, Coast Guard, and Army) and also had varied experiences, to include active duty, retired, and reserve time in the armed forces. Two of the interviews were conducted with staff of para-church organizations that specifically minister to military members and their families. All interviewees had been affiliated with the military anywhere from nine to thirty-one years.

Interviewees Identify Common Temptations for Military Women

When asked from their perspective what the top three or four common temptations that wives of military members face, there was more unity than dissimilarity. The overwhelming majority of interviewees viewed infidelity, whether emotional or physical immorality, as a top temptation. This category would also include the temptation toward pornography of any type. One interviewee stated anonymously:

> You would think that porn is only a problem for men...but that is not the case. Women have their own versions, which include "sexting" on-line or by text with men. The communication is instant and uninhibited and hidden. Another form of soft porn is romantic fiction written for women... women are tempted by the written form of porn as well as the voice of a man...A military spouse at home alone after the kids are in bed and the husband is deep in the heart of Afghanistan or Iraq can find as many relationships on-line or by text and MMS as she wants to find.[40]

The next top category of temptation revolved around resentment, discontentment, and bitterness. Frequent upheaval, constant change, discontent with husband's status or rank, and a myriad of other military situations were alluded to by interviewees in this category. The third top category of temptation identified had to do with unhealthy coping habits. Interviewees noted various responses to the difficulties of military life like going out to bars with "the girls," or being angry and spending the family's funds to get even, or compromising values for acceptance. One interviewee who has been affiliated with the military for almost twenty years put it this way, "...in other words, women trying to

---

[40] Anonymous, interview by author, 2011.

find any anesthetic for them to avoid the deeper issues. Shopping, eating, drinking, partying are some of them."[41]

Interviewees Discuss Military Circumstances That Serve as Context for Sin/Temptation

Interviewees were also asked, "What unique circumstances of the military environment might contribute to or provide the backdrop for these temptations?" As might be expected, the frequent moves, high operations tempo, deployments and short-term assignments that take the military member away from nuclear family were mentioned most often. However, interviewees also keyed in to other unique circumstances that are probably lesser known by those outside the military community. For instance, Sandy and Sue Nafziger, who have served with Cadence International military ministry since 1993, highlighted how the military's tendency toward unit cohesion and teamwork can twist and lend itself to temptation and sin:

> The constant emphasis in the military is teamwork. We work together as a team to accomplish objectives that could not otherwise be accomplished. Therefore, military personnel work together, live in immediate proximity to each other; participate in the same after-hour functions; travel and deploy together, and often socialize together during off-duty time. Then...they begin to involve themselves in sin together...They are away from home in unfamiliar surroundings and have limited or no civilian relationships. When the social/family/cultural boundaries are removed (by being away from home and surrounded by a new standard of morality), the temptations are

---

[41] Julie Carlin, interview by author, August 19, 2011.

> easily given in to. The more they give in...the
> more they accept the new normal. "They have
> all turned aside, **together;** they have all become
> corrupt; there is no one who does good, not even
> one." (Ps 14:3)[42]

Another lesser-known unique backdrop to some of the temptations listed above was highlighted by Jocelyn Green, who married her husband, a former Coast Guard officer, in 2003 and is also the author of *Faith Deployed* and its sequel, *Faith Deployed... Again.* In her interview, she stated the following about how the constant sacrifices military wives encounter can provide an ample opportunity toward bitterness:

> Military wives sacrifice so much for their
> husbands' careers; it can be a daily battle to
> NOT become bitter. They don't get to choose
> where they live, they often can't keep a job they
> love because they move all the time, they have
> to be a single parent, keep everything together at
> home...It's hard! And many times, they don't get
> the support they need.[43]

Ellie Kay, daughter of a reservist military member, retired Air Force military spouse, mother of military sons, and author of several books to include *Heroes at Home*, underscored the unique way in which the military affects the finances of a family as a backdrop to temptation. In her interview, she pointed out that many spouses are underemployed or unemployed due to the constant moving that comes with military life. This "forced" lack of funds can be a context in which wives respond with anger,

---

[42] Sandy and Sue Nafziger, interview by author, June 15, 2011.

[43] Jocelyn Green, interview by author, May 18, 2011.

discontentment, or spending what is not available. As an aside, it is also increasingly evident that many military families live below the poverty line and do not have enough money to make ends meet. Many are eligible for some form of welfare assistance to feed their families.[44] Mrs. Kay also talked about how a limited and fluctuating income can negatively affect military members and their families. Deployment can bring in a higher cash flow due to hazardous duty pay and other entitlements. When families get used to budgeting on additional pay, consequences can be disastrous when that flow stops. Many military members rely on these increases and at the behest of the lure of additional pay, some military personnel volunteer multiple times to go to war zones.[45] War is not only dangerous, but can also be a short-term, lucrative, lure.

Julie Carlin married her husband, who is now retired from the Air Force, in 1994. She is also currently on staff with the Navigator's military ministry and shared how the unique circumstance of the military's performance-oriented system could be the context in which the sin in women's hearts are revealed:

> The military is a performance-driven system, and it is a small community as well...I saw a tremendous amount of competition...There was no limit to what people would do to hurt others' careers or reputations...even Christian women whom I knew would get deceived into thinking

---

[44] See the following articles, Tranette Ledford, "Frontlines and Food Stamps," Military Spouse Magazine, http://www.milspouse.com/frontlines-and-food-stamps.aspx (accessed 8 February, 2012) and an article done by Seth Robins on 15 November, 2011 entitled, "Food Stamp Use at Military Commissaries Up Sharply in Four Years," Stars and Stripes, http://www.stripes.com/news/food-stamp-use-at-military-commissaries-up-sharply-in-four-years-1.160858 [accessed February 8, 2012].

[45] Ellie Kay, interview by author, May 10, 2011.

that somehow their husbands were entitled to
things and then they would make poor character
decisions based on that thinking. I would name
this as the control game. They stopped trusting
God for their husband's career and would take
matters into their own hands, at any cost.[46]

Interviewees Identify How Local Churches Can Help

When asked how local churches can better minister to women in
the military milieu, many interviewees stressed the importance of
further education about the military context and the challenges
military members and their families face. This education could
take the form of attending workshops, to reading selected articles
and books on the subject.[47] Several mentioned the necessity for
churches to identify women associated with the military milieu

---

[46] Julie Carlin, interview by author, August 19, 2011.

[47] The Association of Certified Biblical Counselors (ACBC) may be used as
an educational resource since they now target the military community. Their
2011 annual conference had a military track that addressed several issues
such as "How to Love on Soldiers and their Families," "Post Traumatic Stress
Disorder," "The Theology of Killing: A Just War Theory," "Reaching Your
Community Through Chaplaincy," and "Ministering To and Counseling
Military Personnel and their Families." The Christian Counseling and
Education Foundation (CCEF) also included a session on traumatic brain
injury at their 2011 annual conference that could be applied to the military
context entitled, "Ministering to Those with Traumatic Brain Injuries."
There are several resources that will serve to inform church leadership
and members of the military lifestyle and that also devote pages on how to
come alongside military members and their families. Just to name a few, see
Ellie Kay's book *Heroes at Home* (chapter two entitled "Angels Among Us:
Practical Ways to Help Military Families"), Marshele Waddell's book *Hope
for the Home Front* (chapter 12 entitled, "Serving Those Who Serve: Ideas for
Ministry to Military Families"), or Jocelyn Green's article entitled, "On the
Homefront: Easy Ways to Support Military Wives" which can be found at:
http://www.cbn.com/family/familyadvice/Green_MilitaryFamilies.aspx.

and really getting to know them and what their needs truly are. Chaplain Alex Brown, a Protestant chaplain with the U.S. Army with over 30 years of experience with his branch of service, suggested several ways for churches to be involved. He encouraged churches to do things like sponsor a unit during the holidays, engage with Hearts Apart (a group designed to assist the spouse and children of those left behind during deployment, run by the installation's readiness group) and invite military women into their homes and get to know them. He reiterated that it all really starts with a one-on-one connection.[48]

Sandy and Sue Nafziger, in addition to encouraging local churches to learn more about the military context, also recommended that churches make themselves known to base authorities and to engage military members of their congregations to go back to their base and post chaplains and let them know of their church and the resources it has to offer:

> Most don't understand the unique nature of military culture and the unique problems they face (deployments, etc.). They are not directly involved and military bases are making it harder and harder for them to gain access—so there is very limited opportunity...But...if a Christian Squadron commander or First Sergeant, or Chaplain knows about a qualified, quality off-base resource, they will occasionally refer people. A church that has such a program with available resources should let the local Military Base/Post know by talking to the Chaplains or Christian military personnel who attend their churches. Make yourself known![49]

---

[48] Chaplain Alex Brown and Dr. Delores Brown, interview by author, August 18, 2011.

[49] Sandy and Sue Nafziger, interview by author, June 15, 2011.

Aurelia M. Smith

Interviewees Address the Biblical Counseling Community

The next question posed to the interviewees had to do with what they desired biblical counselors to know about women in the military milieu. The question was, "Do you have anything that you would like the biblical counseling community to know about military women that may enable us to better serve, encourage and equip them to live for God's glory in the midst of their many challenges?" In answer to this question, the majority of interviewees emphasized how important it is for biblical counselors to know their audience. Chaplain Brown shared that biblical counselors should have the same mind-set as a good doctor, in that they should be familiar with what the military does and what their members face (the symptoms) so that an effective diagnosis and treatment (in the form of godly counsel) can be given. Sandy and Sue Nafziger encouraged biblical counselors to realize that, "Single military females form a unique people group with distinctive characteristics and problems.[50]" Along these same lines on the importance of knowing the military audience, Jocelyn Green stated:

> I would just encourage them to try to understand their lifestyle, truly, before dispensing advice. A dear friend is a National Guard wife with a husband deployed, and her church leaders have compared her to a divorced woman and said, "You don't have it so bad, at least your husband is coming home." That isn't a fair or helpful comparison at all...She was also told she would get along well with the single mothers group—again, it's not the same. Being a military wife is its own special life.[51]

---

[50] Ibid.

[51] Jocelyn Green, interview by author, May 18, 2011.

In addressing the biblical counseling community, interviewees also wanted to stress the importance of individual counselors showing their counselees by love and action what right responses to their circumstances looks like. Ellie Kay pointed out that military spouses have numerous opportunities to go and get information all the time (workshops, guest speakers, informational briefings, etc). She encouraged biblical counselors to go beyond informing their counselees about what should or should not be done, to showing them and giving "...feet to what it looks like"[52] in their context.

While compassionate understanding, application, and instruction were frequent messages given by the interviewees in response to this question, a call for discernment and wisdom as applied to the biblical heart was also recommended. Julie Carlin encouraged biblical counselors to not focus so much on the military element that they lose sight of God's work in the life and heart of the counselee, as well as God's call for all His children to focus on loving Him and serving others:

> I think the tricky thing about helping women in the military is focusing too much on the military! I have worked with many young moms in the military who want to blame the military culture for them not taking responsibility for what they need to do and be as they mature in Christ. No matter what the context, a good counselor is going to take that women's current reality into consideration; but in essence, it's about reorienting the young woman towards what God is doing in her life through her military circumstances... it's good for a counselor to encourage young women to get outside of themselves and see the bigger picture. I don't mean to minimize their own struggles,

---

[52] Ellie Kay, interview by author, May 10, 2011.

> by any means, but it's taking those struggles and overcoming the temptation to go places in their hearts they don't want to go with them![53]

Finally, two of the interviewees requested that the biblical counseling community do something further about the specific issues of combat trauma and further training for military women. During her interview, Marshele Waddell recommended that biblical counselors gain further insight into the effects of combat-related problems like Traumatic Brain Injuries (TBI) and Post Traumatic Stress Disorder (PTSD) for the sake of the military members as well as their families. Vast numbers of active duty, guard, and reserve personnel are coming home to their families, jobs, and communities after leaving perilous locations. Biblical counselors should be aware of not only the symptoms, but should have a firm grasp on the reality of who God is in all of His majesty, sovereignty, love, and wisdom as they seek to minister to military members and their families. Cathie Marcolesco, who has been married to an (recently retired) Air Force pilot for twenty years, had a request in another direction that involved strategic training and outreach to military women. She asked the biblical counseling community to train and equip military women in biblical counseling on or near military installations:

> Maybe we need to offer biblical counseling classes to the military women or possibly advertise to them to train military women through base chapels or through word of mouth. I know there are many classes available on-line, but not many women know about them, and more women might be interested in small classes offered on base or near base.[54]

---

[53] Julie Carlin, interview by author, August 19, 2011.

[54] Cathie Marcolesco, interview by author, June 21, 2011.

Cathie's request is an apt call to the biblical counseling community as a whole to equip women to serve each other skillfully with the all-sufficient Scriptures. Equipping women in the military milieu to rightly handle, interpret, and apply the truths of God's Word and bring it to bear on the heart challenges, sins, and temptations this unique group faces will bear blessed, far-reaching dividends for the kingdom of God. These women have access that no civilian pastor or ministry worker typically has and already have the relationships in which to readily apply what they have learned. In strategically seeking to equip these women, we can know that God will take both the gospel of peace and the riches of his Word to places far and wide wherever these women are sent to impact the military in eternal ways.

Chapter 5

The Survey: Christian Women and the Military-Top 5 Temptations

I created "Christian Women and the Military - Top 5 Temptations" and subsequently placed it on-line on 9 June 2011.[55] Respondents learned about the survey via Facebook, personal e-mail, or by face-to-face communication. By 16 October 2011, 114 women took the survey. The survey was open to women who identified themselves as Christians and who were in the military themselves (active duty, reserve, guard, or veteran) or were married to military members. In some cases, survey respondents were both. Appendix A contains a survey summary which includes the original questions and a breakout of participant responses.

Survey Respondent Age Range

The first question sought to obtain the age range of the survey respondents. Respondents had four categories from which to choose. The first category held the eighteen to twenty-five year-old respondents; the second category had the twenty-six to thirty-five

---

[55] I used SurveyMonkey Inc. to create this online survey. SurveyMonkey is not associated with the author, nor does it endorse or sponsor this book. More information can be found at SurveyMonkey Inc, San Mateo California, USA or at www.surveymonkey.com.

year olds; the third category had the thirty-six to forty-five year olds; and the fourth category contained respondents forty-six years of age or older. The majority of women (88 of the 114) reported that they were anywhere from twenty-six to forty-five years of age. In fact, there was an even split of forty-four women in the second and third category. Only eight respondents were in the age range of eighteen to twenty-five years old, while eighteen respondents reported to be forty-six years of age or older.

Survey Respondent Military Affiliation of Service

The second question asked was, "What is/was your military affiliation?" Respondents had eight different categories from which to choose (please see figure 1.1 below). Out of the 113 women who answered this question (one respondent skipped the question), the overwhelming majority of survey takers were Air Force affiliated. Ninety-six of the women responding were affiliated with either the Air Force or the Air Force Reserve. The next largest group (14 out of 113) of female respondents was Army related, either in the Army, Army Guard or Army Reserve. The Navy had six women respondents, the Marines four, and the Coast Guard one.

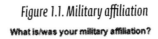

Figure 1.1. Military affiliation

What is/was your military affiliation?

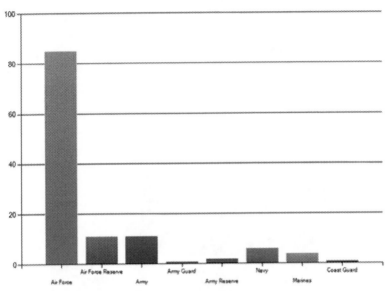

Capacity by Which Survey Respondents were Affiliated with Military

The third question sought to obtain the capacity in which the female respondents were affiliated with the military. This time, however, those taking the survey were able to check all that applied to them. Respondents had four categories from which to select. Twenty-seven women selected the first category, "I am in the military myself." Twenty-nine women selected the second category, "I was in the military" (meaning the respondent is a veteran of the armed forces herself). The third category encompassed the most responses. Sixty-five respondents stated, "I am the wife of a military member." Finally, twenty respondents stated, "I am the wife of a veteran/retired military member." All 114 respondents answered this question, with some women indicating that they were both a spouse, and either currently serving in the military themselves or a veteran of the armed services. The figure 1.2 gives a visual representation of the respondents' answers to this survey question.

Figure 1.2. Capacity of military affiliation

In what capacity are/were you affiliated with the military? Please check all that apply.

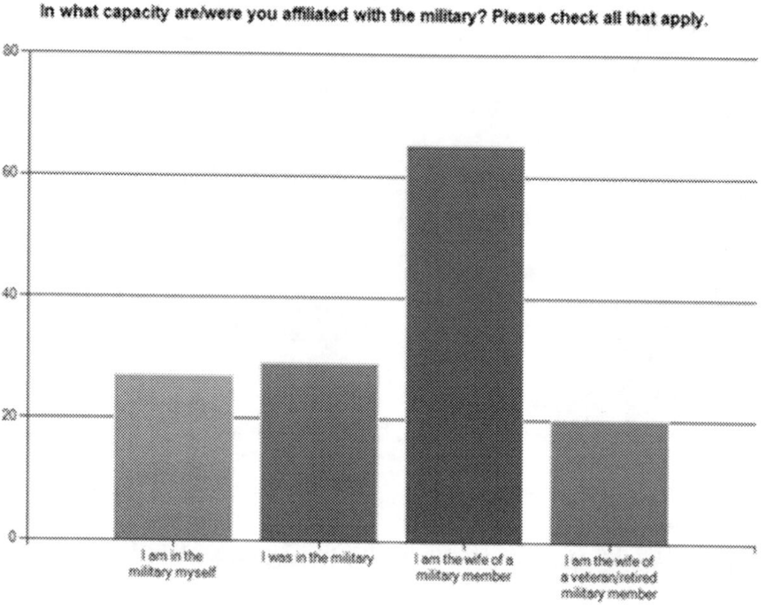

Survey Respondent Length of Military Affiliation

The fourth question in the survey sought to learn how long respondents were a part of the military milieu by asking, "How long have you been affiliated with the military?" Respondents could select from five options that ranged from five years or less to twenty-one years or more. As can be seen from figure 1.3 below, length of military affiliation was more evenly distributed among the categories. Out of the 113 women who chose to answer this question, twenty-one had been affiliated with the military five years or less. Twenty-four women had been affiliated with the military six to ten years. The largest number, twenty-eight women, were affiliated with the military anywhere from eleven to fifteen years.

Twenty-one women at the time of the survey had been affiliated with the military sixteen to twenty years, and finally, nineteen women had twenty-one years or more of military affiliation.

Figure 1.3. Length of military affiliation

How long have you been affiliated with the military?

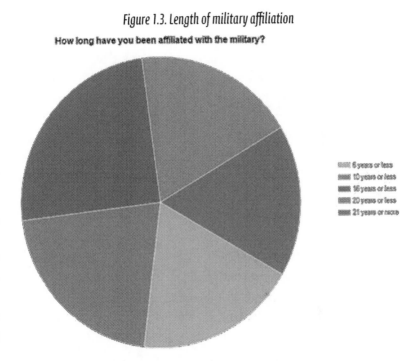

- 6 years or less
- 10 years or less
- 16 years or less
- 20 years or less
- 21 years or more

Ranking of Temptations by Survey Respondents

After attempting to collect demographic-type data, the next two questions were designed to get at the experiences and heart of the respondents by allowing them to list and describe what they perceived as their top five temptations. Question number five asked, "What are the top five temptations you have faced while affiliated with the military?" Question number six asked respondents to share in written form any personal stories or situations that might illustrate their struggle. Fifty-three women were willing to share personal stories that provided a backdrop to their top five rank-ordered votes (their specific details and stories will remain private).

Those who answered question number five had sixteen temptations from which to choose. In addition to selecting five temptations, they were also asked to rank order their selections, with a number one being the highest. Respondents were also encouraged to write in any other temptations they did not see already listed that applied to them. One hundred twelve women responded to this question and sixteen women also provided additional temptations or clarification in the write-in portion.

Figure 1.4 gives a visual representation of respondent answers to this question.[56] Based on the respondents' selections and rank ordering, fear was the temptation selected most often by the women and ranked number one. All kinds of fears were clarified in the write-in portion of the survey: fear of death (member in combat or warzone), fear of not having enough money due to lean military pay, fear of man (being controlled by what peers, subordinates, or superiors might think of the respondent), and fear of spouse being unfaithful while deployed or on military duty away from home. Controlling attitudes and behavior had the highest number of votes for the second top temptation. Women communicated in the write-in portion of the survey that these attitudes and behaviors included trying to direct and superintend difficult times like moves and deployments, as well as seeking to control the family even when their spouses returned from their duty assignments. Finally, the women in the military milieu who took this survey saw bitterness/resentment as their third highest temptation. Bitterness and resentment arose in all kinds of contexts. Bitterness in response to family sacrifices, bitterness at having to sacrifice careers and loved employment due to

---

[56] There are multiple valid ways to quantify the survey respondent data. For this book, I chose to select the highest response recorded by the respondents for the first, second and third choice. Another valid method would be to mathematically weigh the responses, which would produce similar results.

husband's profession, and bitterness at having to be the primary parent were noted in the write-in portion of the survey. Women recorded resentment as a result of long duty hours, deployments, and constant temporary duty assignments; resentment at injustice received at the hands of military peers or superiors; resentment at not being near extended family members; and resentment at not having much choice as to where one lived or raised a family.

Figure 1.4. Top Five temptations rank ordered

What are the top 5 temptations you have faced while affiliated with the military? Please rank order your selection from 1-5.

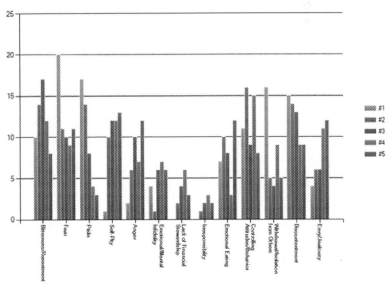

As can be seen from figure 1.4, a number of temptations and sin areas were highlighted by the survey.[57] As was mentioned

---

[57] This simple survey reveals that more work should be done for women in the military milieu to biblically address the temptations and sins represented here. Book constraints such as page limit does not allow detailed coverage of all the temptations seen on this chart. However, it is evident that biblical counselors should prepare themselves to address these issues with their military milieu counselees.

earlier, sixteen women also provided additional temptations in the write-in portion of the survey. Other write-in responses included self-righteousness, impatience, intolerance, sexual immorality, temptations that arise when dealing with unfairness or lack of integrity of military superiors, incorrect priorities, drunkenness or abuse of alcohol, doubt and worry, discouragement, self-sufficiency or self-reliance, coarse talk, and compromising femininity in order to fit in with predominately male (military) peers. Part three of this book will discuss fear, controlling attitudes and behavior, and bitterness/resentment in greater detail.

Survey Respondents Identify Sources of Help They Sought

After respondents rank-ordered their perceived highest temptations and shared personal stories that highlighted their struggles, they were then asked if they sought help in overcoming these problems in the past. Question number seven asked, "Have you ever sought help in overcoming these temptations from any of the people below?" Respondents were given eight choices from which to select and could choose more than one: Chaplain, psychologist/psychiatrist, church pastor, supervisor, commander, ministry leader, friend, or biblical counselor. Ninety-three of the survey respondents answered this question, while twenty-one elected to skip it. There was also an "other" category that respondents could elect to write-in their choice. Thirty respondents chose to provide additional categories of people (or clarification) that were not originally listed.

Figure 1.5 below gives a vivid idea of who women in the military milieu are turning to for help in overcoming these sins and temptations. Those who responded to this survey question reported that they turned to their friends for help the majority of the time. This category received seventy-seven votes or responses and accounted for over 82% of the responses. The next category of people most military women turned to for help were ministry leaders, at only 29% or twenty-seven votes. Psychologist/psychiatrists came in third place, biblical counselors fourth, chaplains fifth, pastors sixth, commanders seventh, and supervisors eighth. The thirty additional write-ins named husbands, God or God's Word, family (relatives), Christian accountability partners or mentors, Bible study groups, or resources like DVDs and books that dealt with the topic of temptation, to name a few. However, out of all these write-ins, none ever came close to the seventy-seven votes for friends. The write-in answer most shared was that of husband/ spouse at a mere seven responses.

Figure 1.5. Source of help sought

Have you ever sought help in overcoming these temptations from any of the people below?

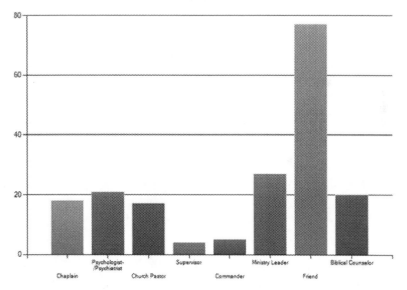

Review, Further Questions and Tentative Conclusions Based on Survey

In review, the majority of the respondents for this survey were twenty-six to forty-five years of age. The overwhelming majority of survey takers were Air Force affiliated, and the majority of respondents tended to be spouses of military members. Despite the fact that length of time affiliated with the military tended to be more evenly distributed, the eleven to fifteen year category had the largest number of women. Several temptations were voted on in this survey and are worthy of further remarks and counsel. However, the top three temptations based on survey respondent identification that will be discussed in future chapters are fear, controlling attitudes and behavior, and bitterness/resentment. Finally, this survey highlighted that the overwhelming majority of respondents turned to friends for help rather than to pastors, biblical counselors, or chaplains in trying to overcome the sins and temptations listed.

With this review of the survey data in mind, what further questions and tentative conclusions might be drawn from this information? First, the age range and the dominating Air Force affiliation of the respondents are noteworthy. Some consideration, and perhaps further study, is needed to see if women from the other services would have identified the same top temptations and sins, and whether certain struggles are more common at different ages in the military milieu. Second, it is readily apparent that the military women who took this survey are predominately turning to their friends for help. What might this say to the biblical counseling community and other organizations that are seeking to equip and train others to counsel and apply the Scriptures with skill? This survey seems to point out that training in biblical counseling should be directed not only at chaplains, pastors, and layleaders, but also to military-affiliated women en masse. In doing so, these particular women will be more equipped to not just give well-meaning, experiential advice or share their feelings and perceptions. Instead, they will be able to shed biblical light on the challenges and heart responses of their sisters in arms and grant them true hope while pointing them to the Person of Christ.

Chapter 6

Fear: Day and Night in Its Cold Grip

In previous chapters, the blessings and challenges of military life were described. The poignant observations recorded from interviews of those who minister to military members and their families were shared. Interviewees gave us their perspective on the military culture and its common temptations, how they believe churches can assist in ministering to military women, and even shared what they desired for biblical counselors to know about this community. Information gleaned directly from military spouses, female veterans, and female active duty members were also presented. These women gave voice to the scenarios, challenges, and temptations that they face on a daily basis in their milieu.

It is evident from what was covered previously that the military milieu is quite distinct from civilian life and that it brings with it some unique circumstances. However, according to Scripture, the women who operate in the military milieu share common bonds with all of humanity in the source of their temptation, the progression of all temptation and sin, and the universal commonality of sin. As such, women in the military milieu are not beyond the help and hope of Christ, nor the life-giving, sufficient, Word of God. James 1:13-15 states:

> When tempted, no one should say, "God is tempting me." For God cannot be tempted by evil, nor does he tempt anyone; but each one is tempted when, by his own evil desire, he is dragged away and enticed. Then, after desire has conceived, it gives birth to sin; and sin, when it is full-grown, gives birth to death.

From these verses, several points are apparent. First, God is not the source of any evil or temptation. Second, the source of all human sin has to do with the inner working of the heart and its desires and not the difficult context or circumstances in which it operates. Third, the progression of sin, from initial desire to spiritual death, is always the same and is common to all mankind.

In a similar vein, 1 Corinthians 10:13 reminds believers about the universal nature and commonality of temptation:

> No temptation has seized you except what is common to man. And God is faithful; he will not let you be tempted beyond what you can bear. But when you are tempted, he will also provide a way out so that you can stand up under it.

According to this verse, temptations and sins are common to the entire human race, despite the context in which they arise. First, no matter how isolated a woman in the military milieu may feel in the midst of her struggles, this verse assures her that she is not alone in her temptations. Other believers have faced them before and her heart responses to these difficulties are not new to God. Second, God is faithful in the midst of her difficulty and is worthy of complete confidence, trust, and belief. Third, God always provides a way to honor Him in the midst of any trial and temptation. If the woman in the military milieu believes what God says through His Word, and looks for the way out that He promised by walking in obedience, she will indeed glorify her Lord in any circumstance.

Finally, Christian women in the military milieu should be reminded that not only do they have something in common with all believers in regard to temptation, its source and its progression (if they do not take the way out God provides), but that the "eternal priesthood of the God-Man" has direct implications on their way of life.[58] They have a high priest who is sympathetic to their plight. In fact, this high priest was made like them in every way. He knows their weaknesses and became like them by taking on flesh, suffering when He was tempted so that He could help those who are also tempted (Heb. 2:17-18). Hebrews 4:15 says, "For we do not have a high priest who is unable to sympathize with our weaknesses, but we have one who has been tempted in every way, just as we are--yet was without sin." It is to this Savior, Mediator, High Priest, and Lord that Christian military women must turn for help, realizing that Christ became a man just like them and is uniquely qualified to assist them, because He never once yielded to temptation or sin. Christian women in the military do not need to invent newfangled answers and strategies to overcome their sins and temptations, despite the unique nature of their operating environment. Instead, the true need is for a biblical view, interpretation, and solution to their problems so that they can respond in God-honoring ways in the midst of whatever difficult circumstances come their way in the military context.

With these truths in mind, this third section of the book will hone in on the top three temptations or sin areas as identified in the on-line survey created during the data gathering phase for this book. This chapter will discuss the temptation and sin of fear. Chapter six will discuss the temptation and sin of controlling attitudes and behavior. Chapter seven will focus on

---

[58] Elyse M. Fitzpatrick and Jessica Thompson, *Give Them Grace: Dazzling Your Kids With the Love of Jesus*, (Wheaton Illinois: Crossway, 2011), 85.

the temptation and sin of bitterness and resentment. Each one of these chapters will be presented in four parts. First, an example in the form of a case study in the military context will be shared. Second, the secular/psychological solutions to this problem will be highlighted. Third, the biblical and theological solutions to the problem will be presented. This solution will consider how one's union with Christ, the Person of Christ, and the gospel impacts the problem. It will also include key passages from Scripture, and touch on how one may need to change in thought, word, and deed by God's grace. Fourth, homework assignments and resources will be presented for each of the three problematic sin areas so that those who come alongside military women with encouragement and counsel will have a resource ready to use in their ministry.

Case Study A: Day and Night in the Cold Grip of Fear...

Amanda[59] jerked awake again with a racing heart and in a cold sweat. The dream was back. The frightful images and sounds from her nightmare of a war zone were imprinted on her mind's eyes and ears. Do what she might, the piercing cry of her beloved husband in pain from her dream stayed with her. Her husband, Adam, was on his fourth deployment to a data masked (classified) location and communication was sparse to virtually nonexistent. Two years before, an Improvised Explosive Device (IED) wounded him. The IED wrought savage scars around his face, hands, and upper torso. By God's grace, Adam had survived, although one of his friends had not. But after months of reconstructive surgery and physical therapy at Walter Reed Medical Center, Adam was back in harm's way. Amanda lay awake as alarming thoughts whirled and spun around in her mind, and she felt powerless to stop them. Not only were her nights steeped in all-absorbing fear,

---

[59] Amanda is a purely fictitious character created for the purpose of realistically illustrating the sin and temptation of fear in the military context.

but her days were assailed with grim imaginations and countless "What if?" scenarios. Amanda lived in a constant state of dread that Adam might never return or that if he did, his wounds would be even more extensive than the first time. How could she go on without her husband? What would happen to her children if they were left fatherless? What if he returned, but came back without the aid of his limbs, vision, or ability to function?

Both Amanda and Adam were Christians. Amanda even knew from 1 John 4:18 that "perfect love casts out all fear" and that fear was not to rule her. She faithfully attended a local church, went to Protestant Women of the Chapel and Military Fellowship events, talked about her struggles with other military wives, and prayed with fervency, but the awful fears still loomed. Her lack of sleep at night was beginning to affect her days as she sought to fill the many roles and gaps required of her in Adam's absence in sheer exhaustion. She could also see that her vigil of fear was negatively affecting her children. Though relatively young, they could sense something was wrong with their mommy who was more jumpy when the phone rang, or turned pale when an unidentified car pulled into their cul-de-sac.[60] Worse yet, Amanda was not able to offer them any firm and soul-grounding hope when they came to her with their own fears and nightmares, as children will do when their daddy is deployed in harm's way. Amanda is crumbling and knows she needs help with these persistent, crippling, sleep-depriving, joy-robbing fears and resolves to ask her women's leader at church for a recommendation for a counselor in her area.

---

[60] When a military member is killed in the line of duty, the spouse, as next of kin, will be notified by a team of officials from the military installation. Hence, Amanda is leery of any unidentified cars entering the near vicinity of her home that might bear bad tidings. If a military member is wounded in the line of duty, the spouse could be notified via telephone about the incident. She is therefore startled at the sound of the phone, frightened of receiving bad news about Adam.

Aurelia M. Smith

Secular/Psychological Solution to Fear

What might be some solutions offered by the secular world? If Amanda elects to navigate the popular culture and tap into the guidance society has to offer, a veritable cornucopia of self-help resources will inevitably vie for her attention. Talk shows, radio programs, magazines, and numerous books claim to enable their adherents to conquer worry and banish fear and anxiety with finality. They promise "Remedies that work"[61] and state their "proven techniques have helped millions to adopt new mental attitudes that lead to security and happiness, teaching them to break the worry habit-forever."[62]

If Amanda instead elects to adhere to the secular counsel of well-meaning loved ones and friends, what else might she hear? If she shares her struggles with other seasoned military spouses, she might get a litany of advice that centers around the importance of keeping busy. "Don't give yourself time to think about it." "Dive into extra activities like volunteering or starting a new hobby!" "Go back to school and further your education." "Travel and see something new!" While nothing is inherently wrong with these suggestions, this "busy" solution still does not deal with the heart and root of Amanda's fears and desires. It may mask the pain and fear temporarily, but it is not a lasting solution. At some point, Amanda will be alone with her thoughts and be stuck with her fears again.

If one transitions from the popular, self-help culture and the well-intentioned advice of friends, what does the more substantial realm of licensed psychology and psychiatry have to say about the

---

[61] Edward M. Hallowell, M.D. *Worry: Controlling It and Using It Wisely*, (New York: Pantheon Books, 1997), 237-306. Part III of Dr. Hallowell's book encompasses his eight step comprehensive solutions to worry and is entitled "Remedies That Work."

[62] Dale Carnegie, *How to Stop Worrying and Start Living: Time-Tested Methods For Conquering Worry*, (New York: Pocket Books, 1984), i.

diagnoses and treatment of someone like Amanda who is being negatively affected, both day and night by her fears of a loved one being injured or dying? The mental health field has many solutions to this type of anxiety or persistent worry. This book will focus on three possible cross-sections of the health and mental health professions: doctors or primary care health providers, psychiatry, and those who specialize in talk therapy (psychologist, therapist, counselor, etc). One important fact to keep in mind while reading this section of the book is that the solutions offered by the mental health profession will depend heavily on the schooling, philosophy and background of the practitioner.

The Primary Care Provider

Let us say that Amanda goes to her assigned Military Treatment Facility (MTF) for a regularly-scheduled medical appointment with her primary care physician. If she decides to mention her persistent fears and her lack of sleep at night in the course of her examination, her doctor will most likely seek to alleviate her suffering in some way. However, because the physician is most likely pressed for time, and is not specialized in any particular field of mental health, Amanda's diagnosis may be vague, and a focus on pharmacology and biology will most likely be the result. One mental health professional put it this way,

> ...the diagnosis would likely be vague...because the primary care physician does not specialize in this area. The treatment would very likely be pharmacological, such as an antianxiety med, an antidepressant, and a sleep inducer... and quite possibly some combination. The physician may not be wholly operating out of a biological model when it comes to etiology, but the reality is that

time constraints force her/him to function like biology is the main issue.[63]

The Psychiatrist

If Amanda sees a psychiatrist, she may attain a higher level of refinement as regards to her diagnosis, but it is quite likely that the treatment would be similar. For example, the psychiatrist may diagnose her with generalized anxiety disorder, panic disorder, or even Post Traumatic Stress Disorder (PTSD). But for the sake of space constraints in this book, let us suppose that the psychiatrist gives Amanda a diagnosis of generalized anxiety disorder. The *Diagnostic and Statistical Manual of Mental Disorders,* or DSM-IV-TR, has the following to state about the features and criterion of generalized anxiety disorder:

> The essential feature of Generalized Anxiety Disorder is excessive anxiety and worry (apprehensive expectation), occurring more days than not for a period of at least 6 months, about a number of events or activities (Criterion A). The individual finds it difficult to control the worry (Criterion B). The anxiety and worry are accompanied by at least three additional symptoms from a list that includes restlessness, being easily fatigued, difficulty concentrating, irritability, muscle tension, and disturbed sleep (Criterion C).[64]

---

[63] Mental health care professional, e-mail communication to author, 1 April 2012.

[64] American Psychiatric Association, *Diagnostic and Statistical Manual of Mental Disorders DSM-IV-TR Fourth Edition (Text Revision),* (Arlington: American Psychiatric Association, 2000), 472.

If Amanda decides to proceed under the care of her psychiatrist, she will most likely be given

> ...some mixture...of antianxiety medications, antidepressants and sleep aids. For many psychiatrists, the biological model of etiology will be more ideologically adhered to. Counseling may or may not be recommended. Follow ups will be mainly concerned with symptom management and side-effect assessment.[65]

While the description of symptoms from the *DSM-IV-TR* may accurately describe her suffering and while the prescribed medications will probably alleviate or lessen her symptoms, they still do not address her spiritual heart and its motivations. Nancy Leigh DeMoss, in the forward of the book entitled, *Will Medicine Stop the Pain?* similarly states, "They may be 'managing' their pain, but they are not experiencing the grace of God to get to the heart issues that may have produced that pain."[66] Amanda will have a diagnostic code and will be given nomenclature to label her experience, but as a Christian, she will want to examine more deeply in the light of Scripture the direction of her worship and the desires of her heart. As a believer, her primary motivation must not be pragmatic relief of her suffering, but rather the glory of God and a desire to grow in Christlikeness.

---

[65] Mental health care professional, e-mail communication to author, 1 April 2012.

[66] Elyse Fitzpatrick and Laura Hendrickson, M.D. *Will Medicine Stop the Pain?: Finding God's Healing for Depression, Anxiety & Other Troubling Emotions,* (Chicago: Moody Publishers, 2006), 10.

The Psychologist/Talk Therapist

What if Amanda decides to see a secular counselor instead? If she goes this route, many avenues would be open to her. Each military installation has programs in place by which military members and their families can access some form of free counseling services through their readiness centers. However, there are myriads of directions that talk therapy, or counseling psychology, can go simply because it is based on the system of thought or particular psychology the practitioner chooses to adopt at any given moment.

Nevertheless, for the sake of brevity, let us suppose that Amanda goes to a psychologist who utilizes some form of behavioral-cognitive therapy.

> The success of this approach centers on the client's understanding that symptoms are a learned response to thoughts or feelings about behaviors that occur in daily life. The client and therapist identify the target symptoms and then examine circumstances associated with the symptoms. Together, they devise strategies to change either the cognitions or behaviors...[67]

Under this framework, the psychologist may decide to work with Amanda using a strengths-based perspective.[68] This means helping a client identify and appreciate positive aspects of her life and to draw from those resources to help resolve what is upsetting her. Here, the counselor would engage in the task of helping

---

[67] Katherine M. Fortinash and Patricia A. Holoday Worret, *Psychiatric Mental Health Nursing*, 3rd ed, (Saint Louis: Elsevier Mosby, 2004), 192.

[68] Psychology Practitioner, e-mail communication to author, 21 March 2012. I owe the strengths-based perspective example in this book to a counseling psychologist who was willing to examine my scenario and make applicable comments.

Amanda reframe her situation as being "normative." Hence, it would be abnormal to not be experiencing pain and discomfort in the midst of her circumstances. The counselor would also work to help Amanda identify resources and strengths in her life that she can mobilize to assist in her times of trial. Her belief in God, her family, and even support groups with other deployed spouses may be social supports used in the process to help resolve what is upsetting Amanda. In addition to this, the counselor would most likely help Amanda identify what is changeable and what is not changeable in her current situation and come to terms of acceptance with her circumstances.

Contrast that with a counselor who, secondary to behavioral research, may encourage Amanda to dedicate a specified amount of time each day to worrying. A counselor influenced by this behavior therapy technique would believe that moderate amounts of fear and worry can actually be comforting, useful, and positive.

> We know from fear research that repeated exposure to feared situations can lessen fear of those situations. In learning-theory terms, repeated exposure to an unrealistically feared event, without anything bad actually happening, results in the "extinction" of the previously learned association of that event with danger. Many phobic disorders can now be successfully treated by using behavior-therapy techniques that depend on extinction.[69]

Here the counselor would work with Amanda to help her decide for herself "what constitutes an appropriate amount of time

---

[69] Thomas D. Borkovec, "What's the Use of Worrying? A Half-hour of Dedicated Fretting Can Help You Chase Away Insomnia, Indecision and That Uncontrollable Stream of Insidious Thoughts." *Psychology Today*, December 1985, 58.

and energy to spend on worrying."[70] Hence, by this view, Amanda would brood for set amounts of time each day under the hope that she could somehow anesthetize herself from the constant stream of fearful thoughts assailing her the rest of the day and night.

Amanda has a large and important choice to make in terms of whose counsel she seeks to help overcome her problem. The ramifications of listening to the voice of popular self-help, well-meaning advice of loved ones and friends, her health care provider, and mental health professionals can have serious and alarming effects on her spiritually and physically.[71]

Biblical and Theological Solutions to Fear

What comfort and practical wisdom might the Scriptures grant to a fear-saturated woman like Amanda? Does the Bible speak adequately to a wife's terror of losing her husband as he performs his military duties? What implications do the Person of Christ and the gospel have on Amanda's problems? Are the Scriptures truly sufficient for Amanda's complicated fear problem? The following pages of this chapter will highlight what God has to say about Amanda's responses to her circumstances and will give a radically different diagnosis and solution to overcoming her pernicious fears.

---

[70] Ibid.

[71] The book, *Will Medicine Stop the Pain?* by Elyse Fitzpatrick and Laura Hendrickson, M.D. is a powerful and helpful resource for anyone to consider regarding the use of medications for emotional problems. This practical resource faithfully considers from a scriptural as well as a biological perspective our bodies, emotions, and the problem of suffering. Chapter six entitled, "Casting All Your Anxiety on Him," is <u>extremely</u> well done and an appropriate place to turn for anyone struggling with fear and anxiety.

How The Gospel and Union with Christ Impact Sinful Fear

What type of impact should the gospel of Jesus Christ have on the fear that Amanda is experiencing? Starting here will remind Amanda that she is already equipped with the power and grace of God through Christ, necessary to carry out the practical work of change. Because of what Jesus has already perfectly accomplished, Amanda can move from being a woman of fear to one of faith and loving trust.

The good news of Jesus' life, death, burial, resurrection and ascension should radically transform the thoughts that Amanda allows in her mind. Jesus died to set Amanda free from her slavish fear of death (Heb. 2:14-15; 1 John 4:18). For the believer, the sting of death is gone because of Christ's work on the cross (1 Cor. 15:54-57). The resurrection of Christ attains for her a living hope of an incorruptible inheritance kept in heaven for her (1 Pet. 1:3-4). Even as she contemplates the potential loss of her husband Adam, these same truths should saturate her fears and turn them to praise. Her husband, and brother in Christ, is destined to be with his Lord should he leave this earth before she does.

The Apostle Paul's words of encouragement to the Thessalonians about those who "have fallen asleep" in the Lord should remind her to not prematurely grieve without hope prior to Adam's passing, nor grieve without hope should he indeed go to be with his Savior (1 Thess. 4:13-18). Through meditating on the gospel and all of its gracious benefits on both her and Adam's behalf, Amanda will focus less on a possible temporal loss and more on the treasure and delight stored up for her eternally in heaven, where both she and Adam will receive the goal of their faith, the salvation of their souls (1 Pet. 1:9).

The gospel of Christ should also be a balm to Amanda's soul when she fails to respond to her fears biblically. She should recollect that the sacrificial death of Christ covered all of her sins in the past, in the present, and in the future. There is no longer any condemnation for her in Christ (Rom 8:1). As such, she stands in the grace of God, with Jesus' perfect record of righteousness, as if she had always obeyed and trusted the Father perfectly (2 Cor. 5:21; Rom 1:17; 1 Cor 1:30). When she does sin, she can know with perfect assurance that God is for her, that God loves her, and that God sees the perfect record of his Son when he looks at her. Hence, Amanda can enter boldly into the throne room of grace and confess her sins of anxiety, worry, and fear, knowing that God will cleanse her from all her unrighteousness when she comes to Him in repentance (Heb. 4:16; 1 John 1:9).

How might Amanda's union with Christ help transform the way she thinks about and interprets her earthly fears? In defining what union in Christ means, Wayne Grudem states the following:

> Union with Christ is a phrase used to summarize several different relationships between believers and Christ, through which Christians receive every benefit of salvation. These relationships include the fact that we are in Christ, Christ is in us, we are like Christ, and we are with Christ.[72]

So then, Amanda's thinking should be radically transformed as she considers the impact of her being in Christ, Christ being in her, her being like Christ, and her being with Christ. When tempted to yield to sinful fear by day or by night, Amanda can know with certainty as a result of her union with Christ that she has a powerful advocate in heaven interceding on her behalf (Rom. 8:27, 34; Heb. 7:25). When jolted awake by fearful dreams, or when tempted to allow her anxious thoughts to rule her days, she can remember the fact that her Lord intercedes for her and that the Spirit intercedes in perfect accordance with the will of God. Second, she can bring to mind the fact that as a result of

---

[72] Wayne Grudem, *Systematic Theology*, (Grand Rapids: Zondervan, 1994), 840.

being "in Christ," God will use every circumstance in her life to further conform her into the image of the Son (Rom. 8:28-30; James 1:2-4). Neither trouble nor death can separate Amanda from the love of Christ (Rom. 8:35-39)! In fact, God has promised to use whatever comes into her life for her ultimate good and His glory. Third, union with Christ makes Amanda not only an heir, but also a treasured, loved daughter of the Most High God. According to Scripture, both Amanda and Adam have received a spirit of sonship (Rom. 8:15-17). Rather than being a slave to fear, Amanda can cry out to her "Abba" Father, knowing that whatever sufferings in Christ she shares, she will also share in His future glory.

Key Passages from Scripture

Psalm 139:1-18 should go a long way to remind Amanda of God's omniscience, omnipresence, and great sovereignty in her life and the life of her husband. Second Corinthians 10:3-5 and Philippians 4:4-9 will give Amanda a whole new understanding of the role she should play in taking her fearful and anxious thoughts captive.

There are three realities about God in Psalm 139:1-18 that can expel fears and bring great comfort to Amanda. The first reality that Amanda must be reminded of from Psalm 139 is of God's all-surpassing and perfect *knowledge*. In verses 1-4, the psalmist writes about the intimate, personal knowledge that God has for him. All of his movements, thoughts, and words are known to his Heavenly Father before they are even brought about. The reality of God's perfect and intimate knowledge should encourage Amanda, since God knows the very thoughts that are troubling her, when she stirs or rises in the night, and even knows the prayers she may utter for help before they are on her tongue. It should also remind her of the fact that although she does not know what her husband is doing moment by moment, God does.

The second reality that Amanda must be reminded of from Psalm 139 is of God's continual and abiding *presence*. Verses 5-12 make it crystal clear that God is in any and every location. Neither Amanda nor her husband, Adam, can escape from His continual and abiding presence. This should give Amanda great hope and comfort as she meditates on the fact that God is present not only with her, but that God is present to bless and protect her husband Adam all the way across the world at his place of duty.

The third reality that Amanda must be reminded of from Psalm 139 is of God's sovereign and loving *involvement*. Not only is God all-knowing and present in every location, but He is also lovingly involved in the details of the lives of His people and in all of creation. Verses 13-16 detail the amazing way God is involved in the creation of human life, and states that every single day is already known and planned perfectly by the Father before one of them even comes into existence. The reality of God's sovereign involvement should give Amanda great comfort because not only is God lovingly involved in every detail of the psalmist's life, but he is lovingly involved and bringing about His purposes in her life and in the life of her husband Adam as well. She can rest assured that absolutely nothing will occur to her or her husband that is outside of God's sovereign and loving plan. As Amanda meditates on the intimate knowledge, abiding presence, and sovereign involvement of our Great God, her terror and fear should give way to great praise, awe, and trust of our King who lovingly reigns on High.

Not only must Amanda be reminded about who God is and what he does from Psalm 139, but she also must be taught how to think biblically and know what to do with the fearful and anxious thoughts that arise day and night. Second Corinthians 10:3-5 and Philippians 4:4-9 will equip Amanda for the battle that rages in her spiritual mind. There are three concepts that are essential for Amanda to grasp from 2 Corinthians 10:3-5. Although the immediate context of this passage is dealing with

Paul's apostolic authority[73] and his defense of the gospel from false teachers and error in Corinth, principles from these verses can also assist Amanda in overcoming her fear and learning how to think biblically. First, Amanda must know that she is called as a Christian to use different *tactics* than those of the world in this midst of this battle of fear (2 Cor. 10:3). As a believer, Amanda must be made aware of the fact that the way she approaches problems, fears, and anxieties is to be completely different than the way of the world. Where the world seeks to deny, "whistle in the dark," think positive thoughts, or medicate into oblivion fears and anxieties, believers are called to fight on an altogether different plane with the sufficient resources God gives by the indwelling Holy Spirit and the perfect Word.

Second, Amanda must know that the weapons God gives her to fight this battle of fear are divinely *effective* (2 Cor. 10:4). Amanda has become entangled and entrapped in a stronghold of fear, anxiety, and apprehension. She must be reminded that although she may feel powerless to stop the onslaught of constant anxious thoughts, God in His kindness, grace, and mercy has given her divine tools that can completely obliterate and demolish this stronghold. These divine weapons will never fail to miss their mark or obliterate the enemy when used in faith and obedience.

Third, Amanda must learn to go on the *offensive* into the fray of this battle for her mind (2 Cor. 10:5). Amanda will want to demolish or transform those thoughts that do not conform to the truth and subjugate the enemy of fear and anxiety to captivity. From this verse, she will learn how to offensively examine each thought that enters her mind. Rather than allow fear and anxiety to germinate in her mind, affect her sleep, and control her life,

---

[73] Dr. MacArthur's outline for the book of 2 Corinthians assisted me in gaining a better understanding of the context and flow of Paul's letter. John MacArthur, *The MacArthur Study Bible*, (Nashville: Thomas Nelson, 2006), 1730.

Amanda is called to destroy them, and then replace those thoughts with thoughts that honor Christ and are subject to His truth.

After Amanda is sufficiently alerted to the battle that is taking place in her mind, her role in the mêlée and the divinely efficient tools and tactics she is to employ for victory, it would be time to teach her Scripture's remedy for the fears and terrors that ail her. The principles laid out in Philippians 4:4-9, which speak of how to handle conflict in a God-honoring manner, are also useful in assisting Amanda know how to replace her fearful thoughts and make them obedient to the Word of Christ in five ways. First, Amanda is to take her fearful and anxious thoughts captive by cultivating a spirit of *rejoicing* (Phil. 4:4). A believer can always rejoice about her Savior, the truth and promises of the Word of God, and in the never-ending love of God the Father. In fact, a continual spirit of rejoicing is a command of Scripture (Phil. 4:4; 1 Thess 5:16). This alerts us to the fact that rejoicing is not primarily based on feelings.

Second, Amanda is to take her fearful and anxious thoughts captive by cultivating a spirit of *awareness* of God's presence (Phil. 4:5). Remembering the truth about God's omnipresence and ability to bless and protect will go far in alleviating her fearful thoughts. Third, Amanda is to take her fearful and anxious thoughts captive by cultivating a spirit of prayer (Phil. 4:6). In place of her anxiety, Amanda is called to voice her gratitude, concerns, and requests to her loving Father (1 Pet. 5:7). Rather than wasting much energy in fear, she is called to entrust all her cares to the God who can actually accomplish good on her behalf.

Fourth, Amanda is to take her fearful and anxious thoughts captive by cultivating a thought life characterized by *self-control* (Phil. 4:8). This means that when her mind reels with anxious "What if?" thoughts, Amanda must by God's grace choose to exercise self-control in her thought life and replace the false and fearful thought with what is true, noble, excellent, praiseworthy, etc. Amanda would have to learn how to do the hard spiritual work of examining each thought that enters her mind, and allowing only thoughts that epitomize these biblical characteristics to remain and to take root.

Fifth and last, Amanda is to take her fearful and anxious thoughts captive by cultivating a life of *holy habit* (Phil. 4:9). As a believer, Amanda's enmity with God is over, and her peace hard won by the body and blood of her Savior Jesus (Eph. 2:13-16). She is held fast by the cords of grace and her reconciliation with God is complete (Col. 1:21-22). However, if Amanda wants to experience all the intended effects of this spiritual reality in her daily life, she will need to put into continual practice what is described in Philippians 4:4-9. Peace here could be defined as "...tranquility, repose, calm; harmony, accord; well-being, prosperity. It denotes a state of untroubled, undisturbed, well-being."[74] Her experience of temporal peace is directly impacted by the repeated hard work of conforming her thoughts, prayers, life, and habits to the truth. Just trying God's ways in this regard once or even one hundred times is not enough. Amanda must continue putting into practice these holy habits until they are a norm in her life, and then blessed peace, rather than anxiety and fear, will reign.

Sinful Fear and the Process of Change by God's Grace

Overcoming sinful fear is not an automatic endeavor. Knowing what the Scriptures say about her problems will not act as a miraculous panacea to her fears. Amanda will find that it requires much effort, empowered by God's supernatural strength, to move from fear to loving trust. However, Amanda can be encouraged that God did not give her a spirit of fear or timidity, but rather one of "power, of love, and of self-discipline" (2 Tim. 1:7). As a

---

[74] Spiros Zodhiates, *The Hebrew-Greek Key Study Bible, New International Version* (Chattanooga: AMG Publishers, 1996), 1615. New Testament lexical aid for the Greek word peace or *eirene*.

believer, she has everything she needs to glorify God in the midst of her circumstances.

Since biblical repentance is a key component of change, it is imperative that we spend some time understanding what repentance truly is. A topic such as this warrants its own book and I won't be able to delve deeply into all its various aspects here. However, I have included in Appendix C a repentance and remorse Bible study that you can use personally, or with your military counselee that can help define repentance, gives examples from Scripture about the truly repentant versus the merely remorseful, principles regarding biblical repentance and more.[75]

Biblical repentance is not merely guilt, remorse or regret. Biblical repentance is distinct from penance and man-made efforts to rectify a very real wrong. 2 Corinthians 7:10 states, "Godly sorrow brings repentance that leads to salvation and leaves no regret, but worldly sorrow brings death." The word repent is defined by the NIV Hebrew-Greek Key Study Bible (HGKSB) lexicon as,

> Metanoeo; from meta, denoting change of place or condition, and noeo, to exercise the mind, think, comprehend. To repent, change the mind, relent. Theologically, it means to change one's mind or disposition toward God. More specifically, to repent is to undergo a moral reorientation of the

---

[75] Other recommended resources to address biblical repentance are "How to Help People Change: the Four-Step Biblical Process" by Jay Adams, "Instruments in the Redeemer's Hands:People in Need of Change Helping People In Need of Change" by Paul David Tripp and "True Repentance" an audio session done by Dr. Stuart Scott at a biblical counseling training conference which can be found at: http://store.faithlafayette.org/browse-by-topic/christian-life-and-growth/spiritual-growth-sanctification/true-repentance-audio-cd/

soul in which one acknowledges the error of his
ways and turns toward the divinely prescribed
way of truth and righteousness.

Biblical repentance and hence change begins by changing
one's mind. Dr. Adams describes repentance as "...rethinking
one's behavior, attitudes and beliefs. It is coming to a different
opinion or viewpoint, one so different that it calls for different
thought patterns and a different lifestyle."[76]

True repentance is characterized by an acknowledgement of
sin, a forsaking of wickedness and a turning toward God and his
ways. Through the faithful use of Scripture and by the conviction
of the Holy Spirit, an individual comes to understand that her
thoughts, attitudes and actions are not in conformity to God's
commands. For the Christian who wants to please God, acts in
keeping with repentance should follow (Luke 3:8; Acts 26:20).
Prayer, humble confession, acts of "radical amputation[77]" when
necessary, and a willingness to pursue holiness and put on the
righteous acts God requires are all signs of a contrite heart of
repentance.

So, with all this in mind, how might those who come alongside
to assist Amanda, or Amanda herself, set about this journey to
change? The first step on Amanda's journey from fear to loving
trust involves having a *right motivation* for change. Above all
else, the propelling impetus that drives her must be a desire to
glorify God out of sheer love for Him. First Corinthians 10:31
reminds her that God's glory should be the ultimate view of all
her actions: "So whether you eat or drink or whatever you do,
do it all for the glory of God." John 14:15 states, "If you love me,

---

[76] Jay E. Adams, *How to Help People Change: The Four-Step Biblical Process*
(Michigan: Zondervan, 1986); 142.

[77] I'm not sure who coined this term and where I first learned it! See Matthew
5:29 and Mark 9:43-47 to see the passages from which this principal is drawn!

you will obey what I command."[78] Hence, Amanda's ultimate motivation to change from a fearfully-anxious woman to a woman of peace, joy, and trust must be out of love for God for all He has done and a desire to glorify Him in obedience. If Amanda is merely seeking nights of uninterrupted rest, deliverance from bad dreams, or a desire to be more productive in the daytime, she should be challenged regarding these inadequate motivations. While these things are not sinful in and of themselves, they cannot be her primary motivation as a child of God. Whether or not her bad dreams diminish and whether or not Adam returns home, Amanda can still lovingly obey God and seek to glorify Him.

The second step in Amanda's passage from fear to loving trust involves *a right understanding of a facet of biblical repentance which is the put-off and put-on principle.* Concepts taken from Ephesians 4:22-32 will help Amanda see that change, or biblical repentance, does not merely consist of stopping her anxious thoughts or being a fearful person. True repentance always consists of stopping a sinful behavior, attitude, or thought and putting on a righteous one that pleases God in its place. For instance, in Ephesians 4:25, one sees that true biblical change does not consist of only *putting off* falsehoods, but also consists of *putting on* the righteous action, which is speaking truthfully to one's neighbor. Likewise in Ephesians 4:28, biblical change involves not only *putting off* stealing but also of *putting on* the righteous action, which is working and seeking to bless others by sharing what one has earned. In Amanda's case, she must also come to the realization that her fears have elicited a type of worship that belongs only to her Lord and God.

---

[78] The link between love and obedience is made quite often throughout the New Testament. John 14:21, 23; 15:10, 1 John 2:3; 5:3. Even in the Old Testament, God commanded His people to show love to Him through obedience (Deut 11:1, 13, 22; 30:16).

> All fear, whether it is a generic, low-level worry or an
> overwhelming and out-of-control "panic attack,"
> is a pervasively moral issue woven throughout
> with choices of faith. One has allegiance either to
> the True God or else to innumerable, false ones.
> Fear is a type of worship...[79]

The legitimate fear that belongs to God alone was given to earthly fears. She will ultimately want to repent of the ways she has bowed down in worship to her ideas of safety, refuge, and comfort that are all connected to her earthly husband and then place her hopes and worship firmly back on Christ. She will also want to engage in renewing her mind in the put-off/put-on process. This would be done by repenting of the ways in which she believed her sinful, heart talk and fears, and by replacing those thoughts with a flow of self-talk from the heart that is filled with truth and confidence in Christ. As Amanda repents of her sinful fears, she can be free to grow more in her fear of God and experience all of the benefits that come from doing so.[80] As Amanda grows in her understanding and application of these principles of biblical repentance to her fearful thoughts, words, and deeds, she will see God-honoring change in her life for His glory.

The third step in the process of change from fear to loving trust will require Amanda to *become adept at using spiritual tools* that God has placed at her disposal to overcome sin and temptation.

---

[79] Andrew H. Selle, "The Bridge Over Troubled Waters: Overcoming Crippling Fear by Faith and Love," *The Journal of Biblical Counseling* 21, no.1 (Fall 2002): 38.

[80] Wayne Mack and Joshua Mack, *The Fear Factor: What Satan Doesn't Want You to Know* (Tulsa: Hensley Publishing, 2002); pages 154-166 detail the benefits of fearing God and are a wonderful encouragement to pursue with delight this righteous fear. *The Fear Factor* has since been republished by P&R Publishing and can be found under the title of *Courage: Fighting Fear with Fear.*

As a believer, Amanda was graced with every spiritual blessing in Christ at the moment of her conversion (Eph. 1:3). She lacks no good thing necessary for life and godliness and is able to stand her ground and honor Christ even when tempted by fearful anxiety (2 Pet. 1:3-4). While there are numerous spiritual tools granted to believers by the grace of God, two will be highlighted here. In addition to her union with Christ, the Word of God and the people of God must be tools that are never underestimated in her fight against the sin and temptation of fear. The living and active Word enables her to participate in the divine nature and escape this world's corruption and evil desires (Heb. 4:12; 2 Pet 1:4). Amanda must learn to not only don the rest of her spiritual armor, but she must learn to wield her sole offensive weapon, the sword of the Spirit (the Word of God), with accuracy, skill, and effectiveness (Eph. 6:17). Through the Scriptures, Amanda will find that she is fully equipped for every good work (2 Tim. 3:16-17).

In the process of change, Amanda will also find that the people of God are a priceless blessing in her fight against anxious fears. Upon conversion, Amanda also became a part of the family of God. She is a member of God's household (Eph. 2:19). With God as her Father, she now is in relationship and communion with all of God's redeemed children as her brothers and sisters in the faith (John 1:12-13; Gal. 3:26; 4:6, Rom. 8:15). This spiritual relationship is of profound importance in her sanctification. Amanda is part of a spiritual body, with Christ as the head (Col. 1:18, Eph. 5:23). As such, Amanda will only grow as God intends if she is functioning as He designed, using her spiritual gifts for the good and benefit of others in the body and allowing the individual members of the body to do the same for her (Rom. 12:4-8; 1 Cor. 12:12-27).

In order to move from fear to loving trust in a way that will exalt Christ, Amanda will have to allow her brothers and sisters to come alongside her in her fight against sin as accountability and encouragement in the truth. Recognizing that in the process of "one anothering," God will use the gifts and talents of others to encourage, rebuke, equip, confront, love, and build her up in the faith to greater maturity (Eph. 4:11-16; Heb. 10:24; 1 Thess. 5:11; Gal. 6:1-2; 1 Pet. 1:22). Armed with God's manifold grace, a right motivation for change, a biblical understanding of repentance, and an adept use of the spiritual tools given to her, Amanda can change and overcome her sinful proclivity to fear.

Homework Assignments and Resources on Fear

Those who come alongside Amanda (biblical counselors, friends, loved ones, ministry leaders) will want to not only speak the truth of God's Word to her in the midst of her fears, but they will also want to help her put into practice the truths she is learning in practical ways.

> Biblical counselors want to promote *biblical change as a life-style*; they want to foster the implementation and integration of biblical principles into the lives of people so that they will become *consistently Christ centered and Christlike in every area of life including, desires, thoughts, attitudes, feelings, and behavior.*[81]

The use of homework or practical assignments is a means by which Amanda can obediently implement scriptural truths firmly into her heart and life. Provided below, in no particular order, are fourteen homework assignments that can be used with a woman like Amanda in the military context who is battling fear. It is by no means a complete or exhaustive list, but it is a place from which to

---

[81] John F. MacArthur and Wayne A. Mack, *Introduction to Biblical Counseling: A Basic Guide to the Principles and Practice of Counseling* (Dallas: Word Publishing, 1994), 297.

start. Appendix B also contains an instructional outline that could be used and expanded over several sessions to address the fears she has about Adam being wounded or dying in the line of duty.

Assignment One

Anyone who comes alongside of Amanda must help her identify and remove desires that she has elevated to idolatrous demands in her own heart. For instance, her desire for the physical safety and well-being of her husband is normal and good. However, when Amanda elevates this desire to a demand, or when Amanda believes she cannot live or honor God without her husband, she has turned to idolatry. Useful resources that can help Amanda step through this process of identification and removal are Lou Priolo's booklet entitled *Fear: Breaking Its Grip,* and Elyse Fitzpatrick's book entitled *Idols of the Heart: Learning to Long for God Alone.* Both of these resources come equipped with questions integrated throughout that will help Amanda see her fears for what they truly are and encourage her to worship God more wholeheartedly.

Assignment Two

Amanda should be encouraged to put 2 Corinthians 10:5 and Philippians 4:4-9 into consistent practice. She can do this by first identifying her top ten most fearful thoughts. Once these thoughts are identified, she should be encouraged to write out one fearful thought on the front of a 3X5 card. Each separate fearful thought should have its own card. On the opposite side of the 3X5 card, she should think up a God-honoring and trusting thought that is scriptural to replace the fearful, anxious thought. For instance, on one side of the 3X5 card Amanda could write the fearful thought, "What if my children are left fatherless?" On the other side of the card, she can write something like, "Psalm 68:5 states that I serve a God who is a father to the fatherless and a defender of widows.

Losing Adam would hurt deeply, yet I know that God is the perfect Father and that I and my children will never be separated from Him! I am not going to borrow trouble, but thank God for Adam's life and his involvement and love for his children in the present." Doing this puts 2 Corinthians 10:5 and Philippians 4:4-9 into practice by taking sinful, fearful thoughts captive and making them obedient to Christ and the truths of Scripture. The cards can be kept nearby for when Amanda struggles most.

Assignment Three

Amanda may greatly benefit from a biblically-sound and easy formula to apply to her fears when they strike. Andrew Selle, in his article entitled *The Bridge Over Troubled Waters: Overcoming Crippling Fear by Faith and Love,*[82] provides just such a five-part formula that Amanda can also use. This article will help Amanda name her fears, reverse her fears (by naming the idols on the flip-side of the fear), pray about her desires, surrender her desires, and love God and others no matter the cost. This valuable resource will help Amanda see how another counselee biblically overcame her crippling fears, and will encourage her to apply the Scriptures to her own struggles with hope.

Assignment Four

She should be encouraged to record and communicate her gratitude to God on a continual basis. Amanda can do this by creating a thankfulness list of at least 20 items for an assignment for several sessions. She should write down what she is thankful for in regard to God (His character, provision, etc.) and her circumstances.

---

[82] Andrew H. Selle, "The Bridge Over Troubled Waters: Overcoming Crippling Fear by Faith and Love," *The Journal of Biblical Counseling* 21, no.1 (Fall 2002): 34-40.

Doing this will help Amanda obey 1 Thessalonians 5:16-18, "to give thanks in all circumstances." It will remind her that God is always blessing her, even in the midst of her hardest times, thereby taking her eyes off her fear and placing them firmly on God.

Assignment Five

Amanda's fears can absorb all of her energy and attention, even during the day. She needs practical ways of putting the first and second greatest commandments of love into practice (Matt. 22:36-40). To accomplish this, Amanda should make a list of things that are not being accomplished due to her anxieties and fears during the day (these tasks can be as simple as checking in on a neighbor, encouraging a friend, or playing a game with the children). Next, have her choose one item from the list each day and commit to completing the task. Accomplishing these tasks will help her take her eyes off herself, and start lovingly working for the good of others and glory of God during her waking hours.

Assignment Six

Amanda will want to make a concerted effort to immerse herself fully in the life of her biblical, local church of which she is a member. Encourage her to seek out a spiritually-mature woman who can come alongside her in a Titus 2:3-5 relationship. Not only will Amanda enjoy even greater fellowship from this relationship, but this will foster more focused "one-anothering." This bond will also provide much needed accountability, prayer and encouragement as Amanda fights to overcome her sinful fears.

Assignment Seven

Have her do a personal Bible study on the life of Ruth or Esther (Ruth 1-4, Esther 1-10). God's consistent, sovereign, loving, all-wise character is on display here, as is His provision for a heartbroken mother, a woman in crisis, and a new widow. Ask her to zero in on the trials they faced, the fears that are expressed by various people in the texts, what divine character traits she sees on display, and how God worked in the lives of these women. In the midst of explaining these passages in context, and locating this story firmly within the greater context of redemptive history, also ask Amanda to record how these truths about God are applicable to her current circumstances. Doing these Bible studies should encourage her that the love, wisdom, and sovereignty of God are always at work and that the God of Ruth, Naomi, and Esther is her same faithful God.

Assignment Eight

Have Amanda obtain a copy of Elizabeth George's book, *Loving God with All Your Mind.* The entire book would be of great benefit for her to read and process, perhaps as continuing homework for each counseling session. However, chapter four is entitled, "Thinking the Truth About ...The Future" and addresses her "what if?" tendencies that lead to anxiety and fear. Reading this book or discussing this chapter will help Amanda learn how to practically submit her thoughts to the truth of God's Word.

Assignment Nine

Amanda can read *Overcoming Fear, Worry and Anxiety* by Elyse Fitzpatrick. Within the book, the author will assist Amanda in understanding the source of her fears and God's answers to her fears. Each chapter has questions she can complete to apply what she has learned to her own life. In addition to this, she can also read Chapter 19 in Martha Peace's book and complete corresponding study guide questions from *The Excellent Wife.* This chapter is entitled, "The Wife's Fear: Overcoming Anxiety." Reading and completing the questions will help her identify how fear may be interfering with some of her responsibilities. In addition to this, the chapter will also help her see that fear is often accompanied with other sins. In identifying these, she will be better poised to recognize them and repent of them as the Spirit convicts her.

Assignment Ten

Have Amanda select songs, hymns, and praise choruses that speak to her fear and enable her to remember God's power (Psalm 57:7; Col. 3:16). Have her listen to these songs and seek to memorize them. When she is awakened by fears, teach her to pray, preach the truth to herself, and sing these songs in her heart. Songs like "A Mighty Fortress" and "In Christ Alone" are a great start. Music ministers powerfully to the heart. God-honoring music will simply remind her of the truths of God's Word and it is another way to put Philippians 4:4-9 into practice.

Assignment Eleven

Amanda will want to have applicable Scriptures at her command at any time of the day or night without having to reach for her Bible. As such, she should start memorizing applicable Scriptures like Isaiah 26:3, 1 Peter 5:7, Job 14:5, Philippians 4:6-9, and 2 Timothy 1:7. Scripture memory is crucial in the battle for her mind. God's Word is a powerful antidote to fear, anxiety and worry. Hiding God's Word in her heart will enable her to not sin in her thoughts (Psalm 119:11).

Assignment Twelve

Amanda may want to obtain Jerry Bridges' book *The Joy of Fearing God*. In particular, chapter eight discusses practical ways of how she can grow in the fear of the Lord. She should also complete the corresponding study guide questions. As Amanda focuses on growing in the fear of the Lord, she will be able to cast off her sinful fears, and she will experience joy and peace as a result.

Assignment Thirteen

Amanda would benefit from reading *Courage: Fighting Fear with Fear* by Wayne and Joshua Mack. This book resource discusses both fear of man and fear of circumstances. It also thoroughly equips the reader to understand, know, and live out true biblical fear of God, which is the answer to Amanda's fears. It will also assist her in identifying the difference between natural fear, sinful fear, and holy fear. Questions at the end of each chapter will assist Amanda in personally applying what she is learning.

Assignment Fourteen

Encourage Amanda to read chapter two and thirteen from *The Biblical Counseling Guide for Women* by John D. Street and Janie Street. Chapter two is about anxiety and provides a look at a woman who is struggling in a military context. It also provides faithful instruction regarding repentance and discussion questions at the end of the chapter. Chapter thirteen of the book is about panic attacks. Although Amanda is not necessarily experiencing the physical symptoms attributed to this specific attack, it speaks clearly and biblically to various phases (readiness, resistance and review) she may find herself in. It will give her the tools to overcome her fears for God's glory before she progresses to such a serious physical response.

Chapter 7

Controlling Attitudes and Behavior: Seeking to Control Military Moving Mayhem

Military-affiliated women ranked controlling attitudes and behavior as the second highest temptation in the survey created for this book. As was illustrated in previous chapters, military life is fraught with large scale, life-altering events that come along with service. Frequent, mandatory moves that are not under the control of the service member and her family and perilous duty assignments that separate loved ones are just a few of the circumstances in the military milieu that can make life challenging. Because military members and their families have to submit to and make the best of so many situations not of their choosing, it is not surprising that a desire to be in control is a high-ranking temptation.

This chapter will address this temptation and sin in four distinct sections. First, a fictional character named Brenda who is struggling with controlling attitudes and behavior will be introduced in the form of a case study entitled "Seeking to Control Military Moving Mayhem." Second, the secular/psychological solutions to controlling attitudes and behavior will be highlighted. This section will include a look at the type of counsel or response Brenda might expect to find from friends, family, pop-culture/psychology, the medical profession, and mental health professionals. Third, the biblical and theological solutions to the problem will be presented. This solution will highlight how one's union with Christ, the Person of Christ, and the gospel impact controlling attitudes and behavior. It will also examine key passages of Scripture and show how one will need to change in thought, word, and deed by God's grace. Fourth, homework assignments and resources will be presented for controlling attitudes and behavior so that those who come alongside military women with encouragement and counsel will have a resource ready to use in their ministry.

Case Study B: Seeking to Control Military Moving Mayhem

Brenda[83] knelt down to record another video angle of the European, antique, solid wood, shrank (closet) in her bedroom. She and her husband, Brad, found the shrank when they were on leave together in Thun, Switzerland. The piece held so many fond memories, especially since they rarely were together. As a dual military couple, Brenda and Brad spent more time apart than they did together. Although they celebrated their tenth wedding anniversary this year, only four of those years had been spent under the same roof as a couple with a joint assignment. Even now, as Brenda was preparing for yet another move, Brad was far away on another continent, taking part in a large scale, multinational, joint-force exercise for the next month. By the time he returned, their home would be packed up and they would have two new addresses - apart again. One address was for Brenda, who was off to complete a yearlong, in-residence professional military education in one state, and another for Brad, who was slated to "fly a desk" in Washington D.C. and do staff work for the next two years.

---

[83] Brenda is a purely fictitious character created for the purpose of realistically illustrating the sin and temptation of controlling attitudes and behavior in the military context.

"With all these transitions, it behooves a girl to be organized," thought Brenda. She remembered with chagrin one move in which she failed to adequately categorize and label several boxes from the kitchen while the moving company packed up her belongings. For weeks she hunted for her missing kitchen items (which included her grandmother's heirloom dishes among other things) in her new home. Imagine her surprise when she finally found them disheveled and dirty, collocated with her lawn mower and spare water hoses in the hot, ant-infested, shed! In addition to this, some of her other household items were never recovered, and were presumed stolen.

To prevent a repeat of that kind of episode, Brenda now created a special binder for each move, took a careful line-by-line personal inventory of her and Brad's items, recorded each room and its important pieces in detail with a video camera (so the condition of the items could be clearly seen for insurance purposes), and sought to plan out each detail of the move and its logistics from beginning to end. Despite all these detailed preparations that were taking up vast amounts of time, Brenda found that she was apprehensive about the move and all it entailed. She was easily angered, shed tears at the drop of a hat, and was apprehensive about any "surprises" that might be around the corner during this relocation. To make matters worse, her military duties were not decreasing and were as demanding as ever despite the fact that her peers and chain of command knew of her impending move. With Brad out of the country, and with his move to coordinate as well as her own, Brenda was absolutely exhausted. As she cried herself to sleep one evening, she wearily thought, "If I don't stay on top of the details of this move a catastrophe will happen. I have to get control of this situation! The God of the Bible is a God of order, isn't He? Doesn't it say somewhere that He helps those who help themselves?[84] Surely he would approve of my detailed

---

[84] Brenda is sadly mistaken in this popular phrase. It is not in the Bible at all!

preparations." As a Christian, Brenda knew that something was askew in her life and perspective, but could not pinpoint what that might be. As she sank into a bone-weary and sad slumber, she resolved to seek help in some form for her troubling feelings before the movers arrived in a few short weeks.

Secular/Psychological Solution to Controlling Attitudes and Behavior

If Brenda listens to loved ones and close friends for support, they may suggest a number of solutions to her controlling and perfectionist tendencies. One type of solution involves the art of distraction so as to lessen stress. Perhaps she could meditate, or go get a pedicure when the urge to overly control surfaces. While this may work in the short-term, Brenda's heart attitudes will still be left untouched and the controlling behaviors will rise again. Another solution friends and family may suggest is for Brenda to put into practice some form of living that tries to find freedom in relinquishing responsibility. The maxim, "Let go and let God," is a prime illustration of this type of counsel. This advice recognizes Brenda's unhealthy focus on control and perfectionism and the importance of turning to God, but it does not address the war of worship that is taking place in her heart. Thus, it would fall far short of glorifying God and biblical change. Even more subtle, it will teach Brenda to view God as a means to her personal end for temporal tranquility so that she does not have to rightly deal with the source of her desires and stress.

If Brenda were to look to the self-help, popular culture, what type of counsel might she find to overcome her controlling tendencies? Both self-esteem and self-trust are popular solutions to a myriad of problems, to include being controlling. Dr. Phil states the following in an on-line article,

> If you fear that you may not be able to handle situations you may encounter, the need to be a control...comes in. Most people have more

> resiliency, depth, strength and flexibility than they
> give themselves credit for. This means you. Trust
> yourself to handle all kinds of circumstances.[85]

This philosophy would teach Brenda to look within to find sufficient strength to overcome her troubling controlling attitudes and behaviors. However, the Scriptures never teach that redeemed sinners should look to themselves for deliverance, nor does it validate trusting oneself. Instead it commands wholehearted love and trust of God alone.

The Primary Care Provider

Should Brenda confide in her Primary Care Physician (PCM), it is likely that he will listen to her concerns and ask her to describe her symptoms. He will probably seek to relieve Brenda's suffering coming primarily from a biological perspective. Her anger, tearfulness, and exhaustion may be interpreted as depression or anxiety, and as such, her PCM would probably offer her an antidepressant. While the doctor is seeking to compassionately care for his patient and relieve suffering, his biological perspective and solution still does not address the spiritual source of Brenda's problems. The antidepressant may do wonders for stabilizing her troubling emotions, but as a believer, Brenda will want to go beyond pragmatic solutions to address the root of her controlling attitudes and behaviors and the disturbing fruit it is bearing in her life.

The Psychiatrist

At this stage, Brenda's presenting problems may not be consistent or severe enough to warrant an office visit or diagnosis from a

---

[85] Dr. Phil, "Stop Being Controlling and Critical," http://drphil.com/articles/article/93 [accessed April 17, 2012].

psychiatrist. However, interestingly enough, according to the *Diagnostic and Statistical Manual of Mental Disorders, Fourth Edition, Text Revision* (DSM-IV-TR), Brenda does meet a few of the criterion for Obsessive Compulsive Disorder (OCD), which falls under the category of anxiety disorders. For instance, she does have "recurrent and persistent thoughts, impulses, or images (that) are experienced at some time during the disturbance as intrusive and inappropriate and cause marked anxiety and distress."[86] She also is practicing repetitive behaviors and mental acts in connection with moving that "are aimed at preventing or reducing distress or preventing some dreaded event or situation."[87] In accordance with the DSM-IV-TR, Brenda is also beginning to realize that her behaviors are "excessive or unreasonable."[88] Her repetitive worrisome habits "are time consuming (take >1 h/d), or significantly interfere with the person's normal routine, occupational or academic functioning, or usual social activities or relationships."[89] Knowing that the DSM-IV-TR accurately describes some of her symptoms and experiences might serve as a well-timed warning for Brenda. If she continues to respond to her circumstances and difficulties in the same manner, she runs the risk of worsening her situation and moving farther away from the trust, peace, and joy that is hers in Christ.

The Psychologist/Talk Therapist

Brenda's problem and symptoms are more suited to nonmedical, counseling psychology or talk therapy. Because of this, it is most likely that if Brenda seeks help from someone in the mental

---

[86] William M. Greenberg, MD, "Medscape Reference: Obsessive-Compulsive Disorder," http://emedicine.medscape.com/article/1934139-overview [accessed April 22, 2012].

[87] Ibid.

[88] Ibid.

[89] Ibid.

health profession, it would be from a talk therapist of some kind. Should Brenda choose to utilize her installation's readiness or support center, she would find a Military Family Life Consultant (MFLC) available for free, short-term, confidential[90] counseling sessions ready to assist her. This individual is a civilian, licensed, clinical provider who is trained to provide support for:

> ...a range of issues including: relationships, crisis intervention, stress management, grief, occupational and other individual and family issues. Psycho-educational presentations on reunion/reintegration, stress/coping, grief/loss and deployment are provided to commands, Family Readiness Groups, Soldier Readiness Processing and other requested locations.[91]

Because of the subclinical nature of Brenda's current problems and symptoms, it is highly likely that the MFLC counselor will seek to assist her by addressing issues related to anxiety and depression. It is also likely that "the sessions may be narrowly focused on a problem-driven approach helping her to reframe her thoughts, find more support in her network, and get some

---

[90] According to Military Homefront, confidentiality in this context has one exception. "The only exception to that rule is when disclosure is necessary to meet legal obligations or to prevent harm to self or others. Legal obligations include requirements of law and Department of Defense or military regulations. Harm to self or others includes suicidal thought or intent, a desire to harm oneself, domestic violence, child abuse or neglect, violence against any person, and any present or future illegal activity." Military Homefront, http://www.militaryhomefront.dod.mil/tf/counseling [accessed 22 April 22, 2012].

[91] MHN Government Services, "Military and Family Life Consultant Program," https://www.mhngs.com/app/programsandservices/mflc_program.content [accessed April 22, 2012].

perspective on the current events."[92] In accordance with this perspective, the counselor could employ some form of Rational-Emotive Behavior Therapy (REBT) or Cognitive-Behavioral Therapy (CBT). REBT was created in the 1950s by Albert Ellis and "is based on the premise that whenever we become upset, it is not the events taking place in our lives that upset us; it is the beliefs that we hold that cause us to become depressed, anxious, enraged, etc."[93] Therefore, the goal of this type of psychotherapy is to reduce emotional pain by getting patients to identify and swap their irrational beliefs for rational ones. So how is REBT different from CBT (which was defined and discussed in the last chapter)? Shane Shackford, in his article on the American Academy of Experts in Traumatic Stress website, offers the following to distinguish REBT from other cognitive behavior therapies:

> ...what separates REBT from the other cognitive behavioral therapies is not the goal of attempting to change and/or modify a patient's cognitions; rather it revolves around REBT's philosophical foundation. (Ellis, 1983). According to Ellis and Bernard (1983), the difference between CBT and REBT "is that CBT does not attempt to modify the overall philosophy and assumptive world of clients through the use of disputational methods (p. 9)." Many of the CBT models seem to be more problem driven, while REBT appears to take the position that behavior and/or emotions are simply consequences of the patient's core belief structure,

---

[92] Mental health care professional, e-mail communication to author, 19 April 2012.

[93] Rational Emotive Behavioral Therapy (REBT) Network, http://www.rebtnetwork.org/whatis.html [accessed April 23, 2012].

which then leads to psychopathology (Ellis & Bernard, 1983).[94]

The use of REBT will require the counselor to have Brenda test some of the absolutist statements and thought processes she has. Statements Brenda makes such as, "If I don't stay on top of the details of this move, a catastrophe will happen," would be viewed as implausible and irrational and challenged or disputed. The counselor would encourage her to change her irrational beliefs (that everything depends on her and that something terrible will happen), for rational ones so that she can experience relief. It would also be highly likely that the practitioner will encourage Brenda to lighten her load and connect with others as a means to finding happiness and reducing negative emotions.

Brenda has a weighty theological decision to make regarding what route she will go to find help. The solutions presented by friends, family, popular self-help culture, her physician, and her MFLC counselor will have real consequences in her spiritual and physical life. While some of these solutions do indeed engage and examine thoughts, beliefs and behaviors (not unlike what a biblical counselor would do), they fail to encourage Brenda to live for God's glory, engage her biblical heart, and look to Jesus as the only powerful source for change.

Biblical and Theological Solutions to Controlling Attitudes and Behavior

According to 2 Timothy 3:16-17, "All Scripture is God-breathed and is useful for teaching, rebuking, correcting and training in righteousness, so that the man of God may be thoroughly equipped for every good work." Brenda, and those who come

---

[94] Shane Shackford, M.S. Ed., " Rational Emotive Behavior Therapy (REBT) and its Application to Suicidal Adolescents," http://www.aaets.org/article101. htm [accessed April 23, 2012].

alongside her to minister, can look confidently to the Bible to accurately identify, diagnose, and provide solutions to the spiritual root of her controlling attitudes and behavior. Brenda can trust that the Word of God is sufficient to help her and enable her to be equipped to live in the challenging context to which God in His sovereignty called her.

How the Gospel and Union with Christ Impacts Controlling Attitudes and Behavior

What type of impact should the gospel of Jesus Christ have on the controlling attitudes and behaviors that Brenda is exhibiting? While there are many ways in which the gospel can shed glorious light on Brenda's problem, two will be highlighted here. First, the gospel reminds Brenda that she can rest in the perfect record and righteousness of Christ. Jesus took on her record of sin and disobedience (2 Cor. 5:21; Gal 3:13). He then imputed His perfect righteousness and record of obedience to Brenda (1 Cor. 1:30; 2 Cor. 5:21; Rom. 1:17; 4:25). There is no longer any punishment for her and no condemnation (Rom. 8:1-4). This glorious reality should encourage Brenda to let go of any ways in which she has been trying to attain perfection. There is only One who is perfect and good (2 Sam. 22:31; Deut. 32:4; Prov. 30:5, Psalm18:30; Matt. 19:17). It should also enable her to rest in the grace of God through Christ when she is tempted to work out all the details of her move and life as a means of self-righteousness.

> The gospel encourages me to rest in my righteous standing with God, a standing which Christ Himself has accomplished and always maintains for me...The gospel also reminds me that my righteous standing with God always holds firm regardless of my performance, because my standing is based solely on the work of Jesus and not mine. On my worst days of sin and failure,

the gospel encourages me with God's unrelenting grace toward me. On my best days of victory and usefulness, the gospel keeps me relating to God solely on the basis of Jesus' righteousness and not mine.[95]

Second, as Brenda meditates on the truths of the gospel, she will be best poised to fight pride and nurture humility. Controlling attitudes and behavior reveal a heart that is inclined to believe in one's own power, sufficiency, and abilities rather than trusting in God's power and sufficiency. The gospel is a salient anecdote to this prideful propensity. The gospel will remind Brenda that she was powerless and dead in her sin (Rom. 5:6-8; Eph. 2:1-2, 4-5). It will also remind her of the incredible wrath that God laid upon His sinless Son on her behalf (Isa. 53:4-12; 1 John 2:2). Thoughts like these do not promote pride. Rather, they promote an immeasurable attitude of thankfulness and humility in the heart of the believer as she contemplates the hatefulness of her sin and the great lengths God took to rescue her. In his book entitled *A Gospel Primer for Christians: Learning to See the Glories of God's Love*, Milton Vincent shares the following about how rehearsing the gospel to oneself assists in cultivating humility and dispersing pride,

> Preaching the gospel to myself each day mounts a powerful assault against my pride and serves to establish humility in its place. Nothing suffocates my pride more than daily reminders regarding the glory of my God, the gravity of my sins, and the crucifixion of God's own Son in my place. Also, the gracious love of God, lavished on me

---

[95] Milton Vincent, *A Gospel Primer for Christians: Learning to See the Glories of God's Love*, (Bemidji: Focus Publishing, 2008), 20.

because of Christ's death, is always humbling to remember, especially when viewed against the backdrop of Hell I deserve.[96]

What about Brenda's union with Christ? Remember, union with Christ encompasses our new identity and all the spiritual benefits of salvation. It is the reality of "...the fact that we are in Christ, Christ is in us, we are like Christ, and we are with Christ."[97] How might this spiritual reality impact her problem of controlling attitudes and behavior? First, union with Christ should remind Brenda of His magnificent and never-ending love toward her (John 15:13; Rom. 8:37-39). This knowledge will strengthen her in her fight against sin and propel her toward greater love for her Savior, which will manifest itself in obedience (John 14:15, 21,23; 15:10, 1 John 5:3). The authors of *Counsel from the Cross: Connecting Broken People to the Love of Christ* put this aspect of union this way:

> Our union with Christ should refresh our hearts with joy and strengthen our faith to enable us to fight for holiness. Realizing that he has loved us so much that he has made us one with himself should engender fervent love in our hearts, resulting in fervent obedience.[98]

Second, as was discussed earlier, because Brenda is in Christ, she can know that she has His perfect record of loving obedience and submission (1 Cor. 1:30; 2 Cor. 5:21; Rom. 1:17; 4:25). She is not meant to bear the weight of trying to attain perfection and

---

[96] Ibid., 27-28.

[97] Wayne Grudem, *Systematic Theology*, (Grand Rapids: Zondervan, 1994), 840.

[98] Elyse M. Fitzpatrick and Dennis E. Johnson, *Counsel from the Cross: Connecting Broken People to the Love of Christ*, (Wheaton: Crossway, 2009), 115.

keep everything afloat. Jesus Himself bore the weight, and she can rest in His perfections. Third, because of the indwelling of Christ within Brenda, she can bear much spiritual fruit for His glory (John 15:5,16; Matt. 13:23). This means that in the context of her controlling attitudes and behavior, Brenda has the power and ability to focus on things above and seek out authentic, eternal treasure instead of clinging so tightly to her temporary, earthly treasures (Col. 3:1-4; Matt. 6:19-21). Fourth, Brenda's union with Christ means that she is becoming more and more like Him and is called to imitate him in daily life (Rom. 8:29; 2 Cor. 3:18; Phil. 1:6; Eph. 5:1; Phil. 2:5; 1 Cor. 11:1). Jesus submitted Himself to the will of the Father, lived a life characterized by sacrifice and humility, and endured suffering with His eyes set on the joy that was to come (Luke 22:42; Phil. 2:1-8; Heb. 12:2-3). Likewise, Brenda is to imitate her Savior by submitting to God's sovereign design and details of her life and humbly walking through whatever comes in trust and joy in her certain reward.

Key Passages from Scripture

All of Scripture puts God's sovereignty on glorious display. From creation to salvation to redemption, the Bible in its totality puts His power and ability in clear view. However, for the sake of brevity, James 4:13-16 and Psalm 127:1-2 will be used as key passages to help Brenda better understand how God's sovereignty impacts her problem of controlling attitudes and behavior. Brenda's dread of what may negatively happen needs to be transformed. James 1:2-4 will be the key passage used to help her view trials and the possibility of her worst-case scenario as a means to rejoice.

The original audience for the book of James was Jewish believers who were dispersed abroad (James 1:1), and the epistle contains "a series of tests by which the genuineness of a person's faith may be measured."[99] However, principles drawn from James 4:13-16 can be readily applied to Brenda and her quest to control moving mayhem since it speaks to God's sovereign control over the details of Brenda's life and the importance of humbly recognizing His authority in the making of her plans.

James 4:13-16 condemns presumptuous planning in four ways. First, it addresses those who plan out the details of their lives without thought to God (v 13). While Brenda is not a Jewish business owner circa A.D. 44-49 (the timeframe the epistle of James was written), she is busily strategizing about where she will go and how she will accomplish her business of moving. Also like those addressed in the text, Brenda is planning out the details of her life without thought to God. Dr. John MacArthur in his notes about this verse states the following:

> James does not condemn wise business planning, but rather planning that leaves out God. The people so depicted are practical atheists, living their lives and making their plans as if God did not exist. Such conduct is inconsistent with genuine saving faith, which submits to God.[100]

Second, it points out the brevity and uncertainty of life (v 14). Those addressed in the passage are reminded that they do not have the foreknowledge to make their plans come to life. Nor are they aware of when their brief time on this earth will draw to a close (Psalm 39:5, 144:4). Likewise, Brenda will want to remember that God is the omniscient one, and He knows the length of her

---

[99] Dr. John MacArthur's outline for the epistle of James was very useful in arranging this key passage's context. John MacArthur, *The MacArthur Study Bible,* (Nashville: Thomas Nelson, 2006), 1894.

[100] Dr. John MacArthur's outline for the epistle of James was very useful in arranging this key passage's context. John MacArthur, *The MacArthur Study Bible,* (Nashville: Thomas Nelson, 2006), 1902.

days (Psalm 139:16). Instead of seeking to control that which she is powerless to control, she will want to rest in God's divine knowledge and loving plan for her life. Third, the passage points to the sovereignty of God and instructs all planners to be prepared to yield to His provident purposes (v 15). In accordance with this verse, Brenda will want to plan in humble submission to God's sovereign will. In doing so, she will neither neglect her responsibilities nor assume in pride that everything depends on her for a favorable outcome. Instead, she will prayerfully and carefully make plans associated with her move, trusting that God might override them for her ultimate good and His glory. Fourth, presumptuous plans are equated to the evil of pride (v 16). Plans that are made without acknowledgement of and submission to God are identified as a form of boasting or bragging. Whether voiced audibly or internally as a thought of the heart, Brenda has been engaging in a form of boasting in a spiritual sense. By God's grace, she will want to repent of the ways in which she has been presumptuously planning, forsake the pride it represents, and then humbly submit her plans and the ultimate outcome to her loving Father.

Psalm 127:1-2 may also be used as a key passage in helping Brenda humbly yield and trust in her sovereign God's care. Psalm 127 is one of the fifteen psalms that would have been sung by Jewish pilgrims on their way to Jerusalem for the three feasts commanded by God. So then, pilgrims would sing these collective psalms in preparation for worship of the living God. However, principles drawn from Psalm 127:1-2 will do much to help Brenda see "God's sovereignty in everyday life"[101] and encourage her to remember that unless He builds, protects, and provides, all of her strivings are in vain. First, the author of this psalm, Solomon, highlights the *Lord's sovereignty in building* (v 1). He reminds

---

[101] John MacArthur, *The MacArthur Study Bible*, (Nashville: Thomas Nelson, 2006), 847.

his audience that if God Himself is not the initiator in building a house, those who seek to do so will labor in vain. Though Brenda is not seeking to build a physical house from the ground up, this principle still applies to her. She will want to slow down, take a step back, and evaluate scripturally whether she is truly "building" and laboring where God would desire her to build. If she is not, vanity and frustration will be the result since she will be working at cross-purposes with God. Second, Solomon highlights the *Lord's sovereignty in guarding and watching* (v 1). Here, watchmen are guarding a city with vigilance. However, the writer of Psalm 127 states that despite their due vigilance, time, and attention, it matters nothing if God Himself is not watching over the city. Brenda, in a spiritual sense, is carefully guarding her possessions and seeking to prevent some kind of feared catastrophe from taking place. However, she too must be reminded that all of her careful guarding, planning and vigilance will avail her nothing if God has other plans. Third, the author shows *God's loving sovereignty even over the toil and sleep of humankind* (v 2). Psalm 127:2 reads, "In vain you rise early and stay up late, toiling for food to eat— for He grants sleep to those He loves." Brenda's preoccupation with her move is consuming her time and life. In her early rising and in her late night vigils, she is working with an intensity that is wearing her out. Those who come alongside of Brenda to help her with her problems will want to lovingly remind her to not fight against her Father by seeking to toil when He is directing trust and rest in His provision. While Brenda will still have the responsibility to build, labor, and watch to a certain extent, Psalm 127:1-2 will help her see her utter dependence on God for the outcome.

The third key passage, James 1:2-4, will help Brenda view her trials, both real and imagined, as a means by which God works good in her life. First, Brenda needs to see that a believer is expected to have *joy* in the midst of any and every circumstance (v 2). This is possible because of the indwelling Holy Spirit, union with Christ, the precious promises from the Word, and God's sovereign hands that always work everything out for good (2 Pet. 1:3-4; Rom. 8:28). Second, Brenda needs to understand and trust that God uses her sufferings and trials for *good purposes*, one of which is to conform her more into the image of Christ (vv 3-4, Rom. 8:29). Even if every article of her furniture was broken, stolen, or misplaced, this passage should help Brenda see that those very hardships would be the very things that God will use to develop in her perseverance, maturity, greater dependence on Him, character, and faith. Rather than seeking to control every detail of her present circumstances in the hope of preventing "catastrophe," Brenda must learn to trust God and accept whatever trials He sends as God's "discipline" or "pruning" that will surely result in "a harvest of righteousness and peace" if she will be trained by it (John 15:1-2; Heb. 12:7-11). Remembering the sure profit that is to be gained by even the hardest trials should encourage Brenda to relinquish and repent of the ways in which she has been trying to control this move, and instead trust her sovereign God to bring about all He has planned for her.

Controlling Attitudes and Behavior and the Process of Change, by God's Grace

How might those who come alongside to assist Brenda set about this journey to change? In addition to having the *right motivation* for change that was discussed in the previous chapter, the first step on Brenda's journey from controlling attitudes and behavior to humble trust in God's sovereignty involves *learning more about and rejoicing in God's attributes and character*. While this would include His sovereignty, it would also encompass His love, His wisdom, His mercy, His compassion, justice, patience, eternal nature, etc (Exod. 34:6-7; Num. 14:18; Deut. 4:31; Jer. 9:24; 1 John 4:16; Rev. 1:8). As Brenda grows in her knowledge and understanding of God's character, her love and awe for Him will grow. This necessarily will also lead to seeing His great power and love directed toward her in every detail of her life. It will combat pride, cultivate humility, and foster trust for her great God.

Second, in the process of change, Brenda will want to *gaze long and meditate continually on Christ's perfections.* The New American Standard translation of 2 Corinthians 3:18 states, "But we all, with unveiled face, beholding as in a mirror the glory of the Lord, are being transformed into the same image from glory to glory, just as from the Lord, the Spirit." All believers have the privilege of clearly and without hindrance gazing at the glory and perfections of the Lord as revealed in the Scriptures. As believers savor and behold His beauty, they are also progressively transformed more into the image of the One on whom they gaze. Therefore, Brenda will want to saturate her heart and spiritual eyes with the glory, perfections, and beauty of her Lord throughout the pages of Scripture. As she does so, she will be focused less on attaining some form of perfection in her own right, and be more wholly absorbed in the perfections of her Savior.

Third, not unlike Amanda in the previous chapter, Brenda will also need to *understand and apply the process of biblical repentance.* This will involve putting off ungodly thoughts, attitudes, speech, and behavior and putting on godly thoughts, attitudes, speech, and behavior in their place. In Brenda's case, she will want to put off making plans apart from God and not recognizing His ultimate sovereignty, which equates to a form of ungodliness (James 4:13-16; Psalm 127:1-2). Then, by God's grace and in God's power, she will want to put on God-dependence, humility, and submission to the will of God. Second, Brenda will also want to repent of the ways in which she has tried to pridefully assume God's place and attributes (Isa. 46:9, 55:8-11). Sarah Albrecht discusses the pride and futility associated with trying to take the place of God: "When we try to be God, we will always fail. We will quickly grow weary, and our souls will not be at peace. We feel the burden of the ultimate sin of pride when we think that we can do God's job better than He can."[102] In her heart, Brenda will want to denounce and put off the ways she sought to be God. Then, she will want to put on a humble attitude of submission, confessing her utter dependence on and trust of God as the ultimate sovereign. Third, Brenda will want to repent of any way in which she is treasuring earthly things above Christ. Passages like Matthew 6:19-21 will remind her of the link between her treasure, her heart, and her worship. In light of these truths, she will want to put off clinging tightly to any earthly treasures such as her material possessions or sense of being in control. In their place, she will want to then put on an eternal reward perspective, where she actively stores up for herself treasures in heaven "where moth and rust do not destroy, and where thieves do not break in and steal."

Fourth, just like Amanda in the previous chapter, Brenda will want to *become adept at using spiritual tools* which God in His grace and mercy gave her in Christ so she can overcome controlling attitudes and behavior. In the last chapter, the Word of God and the people of God were especially highlighted. These spiritual tools and means of grace are necessary for Brenda as well.[103] In addition to these, Brenda will want to learn to wield the spiritual tool of prayer effectively. God's sovereignty does not negate Brenda's responsibilities, so she will still have the responsibility to plan, prepare, and carry out what is necessary for the impending moves. However, the attitude and motive in which she carries out these responsibilities can be greatly impacted by purposeful prayer. She will want to pray continually (1 Thess. 5:17; Rom.

---

[102] Sarah Joy Albrecht, "God is Awake," http://www.ccef.org/god-awake [accessed April 22, 2012].

[103] In accordance with becoming adept at using the means of grace God gives us in His people, Brenda should avail herself of the help of her fellow believers in her local church. They can help her accomplish many of the details of what must be done, but they can also encourage her in the midst of the process by their presence, prayers, accountability, love, and even looking for opportunities to evangelize those of the moving staff who may be unsaved.

12:12). She will want to voice her concerns and requests to God (Phil. 4:6; Eph. 6:18). She will want to pray for God's will to be done (Matt. 6:10; Luke 22:42; Acts 21:14). She will want to pray in accordance with the Scriptures (any of Paul's prayers illustrate this beautifully: Eph. 1:15-23; 3:14-19; Col. 1:9-14). She will want to pray in thanksgiving (Phil. 4:6; Col 4:2; 1 Thess. 5:16-18). Arthur W. Pink has this to say about God's sovereignty in prayer:

> ...prayer is a coming to God, telling Him my *need*, committing my way unto the Lord, and leaving Him to deal with it as seemeth *Him* best. *This* makes my will subject to His, instead of, as in the former case, seeking to bring His will into subjection to mine. No prayer is pleasing to God unless the spirit actuating it is, '*not* my will, but thine be done.'[104]

As Brenda prays in this persistent, humble, trusting, thankful, dependent, and submissive way, she will be better poised to receive God's grace in the midst of her trials and find herself relinquishing the reins of controlling attitudes and behavior.

Homework Assignments and Resources on Controlling Attitudes and Behavior

Now that we have considered how Brenda's union with Christ, the gospel, key biblical passages, and the process of biblical change impact her problems, we want to consider how to integrate these truths into her daily life. Provided below, in no particular order, are ten homework assignments that can be used with a woman like Brenda in the military context who is battling controlling attitudes

---

[104] Arthur W. Pink, *The Sovereignty of God* (Grand Rapids: Baker Books, 1930), 173.

and behavior. It is by no means a complete or exhaustive list, but it is a place from which to start. The counselor or friend who comes alongside Brenda will want to take what is provided below and create smaller, measurable assignments for his counselee. Assignments two and three are expanded to give the reader an idea of what this may look like for one session. Appendix D also contains an instructional outline that could be used and expanded over several sessions to address these struggles.

Assignment One

Consider a study in the book of Jonah. God's sovereignty is on astounding display as He uses a reluctant prophet to preach a message of repentance to the lost people of Nineveh. His power over creatures (worm, a great fish), the creation (wind, sea, plants, scorching east wind, etc) and all people (Jonah, sailors, the people of Nineveh from the greatest to the least) are clearly seen here. Brenda will be encouraged to see the power and sovereignty of her God even in the smallest things and should walk away with a firm understanding that He is in complete control over all the details of her life as well, and that no purpose of His can be thwarted.

Assignment Two

Psalm 104 would be an excellent passage on which Brenda could meditate. Within this chapter, God's power in creation and His continued care and provision for all He created (animals, plants and man) declare His loving sovereignty. After considering all of God's mighty acts and power, the psalmist is compelled to erupt in praise, singing, and rejoicing. By God's grace, after contemplating God's mighty deeds and unsurpassed power, Brenda should also be compelled to trust and praise. Psalm 104 could also be used as a text from which Brenda can pick out specific verses to memorize and then pray back to God. For instance, Psalm 104:33-34 state,

"I will sing to the Lord all my life; I will sing praise to my God as long as I live. May my meditation be pleasing to Him, as I rejoice in the Lord." She could memorize these verses, and when tempted with controlling thoughts, recite them back to the Lord as a prayer that transforms her thoughts into praise and asks for His help to dwell on what is pleasing to Him.

Assignment Three

The book *Respectable Sins: Confronting the Sins We Tolerate* by Jerry Bridges may be of great help in Brenda's life. In particular, the chapters on pride and ungodliness would be of important assistance in her journey to overcome controlling attitudes and behavior. Bridges defines ungodliness this way: "Ungodliness may be defined as living one's everyday life with little or no thought of God, or of God's will, or of God's glory, or of one's dependence on God."[105] Brenda has been making presumptuous plans that necessarily involve pride and a type of practical atheism. Therefore, she would be greatly helped by both this book and its corresponding study guide that will help her apply biblical truths to her problem and help her overcome these sins. A detailed, measurable assignment from the book could look like the following: First, Brenda's counselor could assign chapter seven on the sin of ungodliness to read. Second, after reading the material, Brenda could be required to complete the corresponding study guide questions for this same chapter. Third, the counselor could ask Brenda to select one of the "Take it to Heart" items on page 39 of the study guide under personal reflections and use a journal to reflect on her specific answers and applications to her life. Fourth, Brenda could be asked to come to the next session ready to discuss how she implemented at least two of the truths from this chapter

---

[105] Jerry Bridges, *Respectable Sins: Confronting the Sins We Tolerate* (Colorado Springs: NavPress, 2007), 54.

and homework to her life in the past week. All of these specifics would help Brenda more carefully observe what she is reading, and then put it into practice in her everyday life so that she is not just a reader of the Word, but a blessed doer of the Word (James 1:22-25).

Assignment Four

Anyone who comes alongside of Brenda in her fight against controlling attitudes and behavior will want to address the fears and worry that are behind her actions. The counseling outline, key passages, and homework in the previous chapter should also apply in her situation. In addition, other passages like Matthew 6:25-34 can be stepped through verse by verse to highlight the futility of worrying, showing God's sovereign and loving provision and the importance of seeking the kingdom of God first.

Assignment Five

Studying the attributes and character of God will help Brenda see her Father more accurately and spur on a deeper love and reverential awe of His person. A book like *The Attributes of God* by Arthur W. Pink can be helpful to read through and think on. Seventeen attributes of God are succinctly presented in this book. A.W. Tozer's work, *The Attributes of God: A Journey into the Father's Heart,* could also serve this purpose. Concentrating on the character and attributes of God will cause Brenda to place her eyes on her all-powerful, loving, Creator who is working out everything in her life in accordance with His will.

Assignment Six

Since Brenda's controlling attitudes and behavior are a form of pride, true repentance will involve putting on humility. The book entitled *Humility: True Greatness* by CJ Mahaney and Joshua Harris could be a valuable resource in helping her overcome pride in its various forms. Although the whole short book would be profitable to read through, Brenda may want to pay close attention to the sections entitled, "Responding Humbly to Trials" and "How to Weaken Pride and Cultivate Humility."

Assignment Seven

A study on the book of Job will be a great encouragement and fuel Brenda's desire to submit to the will of our Sovereign Lord. In addition to seeing His great power on display, she will also clearly see that trials are brought into the lives of even His most righteous children (Job 1:8). Job suffered shattering, life-altering trials not because of what he failed to do, but because of God's good, righteous, loving, hidden (to Job it was hidden) purposes. This book will show Brenda that regardless of all of her efforts, God may choose to bring or allow trials into her life that are connected with her impending move. However, no trial and no power of hell can come close to her without His permission (Job 1:9-12). Ultimately, Brenda will want to focus on glorifying God if He gives, and glorifying God if He takes away knowing that He is good and wields His power in perfect love and wisdom on behalf of His people (Job 1:21, 2:10).

Assignment Eight

Controlling attitudes and behavior have at their core a crisis of trust. Brenda not only needs to hear about God's unmatched power and sovereignty, she also needs to be reminded of how trustworthy He is. *Trusting God: Even When Life Hurts* by Jerry Bridges is an outstanding resource to help her remember that God is completely trustworthy and in control of all events, including the adversity that comes into her life. This book and its corresponding study guide will step Brenda through God's sovereignty, wisdom, and love in a compelling way and will encourage her to live out these truths through personal application.

Assignment Nine

Brenda will want to work hard with the strength and grace that God provides to put off unbiblical thoughts that are fueling her controlling attitudes and behavior. In order to do so, she will want to put 2 Corinthians 10:5 and Philippians 4:4-9 into consistent practice. Thoughts like "If I do not stay on top of the details of this move, a catastrophe will happen," and "I have to get control of this situation!" must be dealt with and combated head on with the truth. See the previous chapter on how Brenda can use 3X5 cards and conform her thoughts to what is noble, true, right, pure, lovely, and admirable so that she, too, can experience the temporal peace of God in the midst of her situation.

Assignment Ten

Those working alongside Brenda may be greatly helped by stepping through a Journal of Biblical Counseling article entitled *Obsessions and Compulsions: Breaking Free of the Tyranny* by Michael R. Emlet and creating homework based on its contents. While those who have been diagnosed with OCD are the focus, Brenda is exhibiting some of these same criterions. A biblical anthropology, a discussion of potential heart issues, and a ministry approach to assist those struggling with OCD or controlling attitudes and behavior are all included in this article.

Chapter 8

Bitterness and Resentment: Stranded and Bitter in the Far East

Military-affiliated women ranked bitterness and resentment as the third highest temptation in the survey created for this book. This chapter will address this temptation and sin in four distinct sections. First, a fictional character named Connie who is struggling with bitterness and resentment will be introduced in the form of a case study entitled, "Stranded and Bitter in the Far East." Second, the secular/psychological solutions to bitterness and resentment will be highlighted. This section will include a look at the type of counsel or response Connie might expect to find from friends, family, pop-culture/psychology, the medical profession, and mental health professionals. Third, the biblical and theological solutions to the problem will be presented. This solution will highlight how one's union with Christ, the Person of Christ, and the gospel impacts bitterness and resentment. It will also examine key passages of Scripture and how one might need to change in thought, word, and deed by God's grace. Fourth, homework assignments and resources will be presented for bitterness and resentment so that those who come alongside military women with encouragement and counsel will have a resource ready to use in their ministry.

Aurelia M. Smith

Case Study C: Stranded and Bitter in the Far East

Connie[106] vigorously wiped away another tear from her cheek as she looked at her extended family's photo from home. Connie was a small-town girl from the Midwest who appreciated the multifaceted blessings of family and the stability of roots that spanned several generations. The photo was a memento from her great-grandmother's 90th birthday celebration. Connie was not able to attend this joyous commemoration along with her relatives because the cost of airfare from Korea would have been far too high.

For the millionth time, Connie wondered what she was doing in the Far East. Although she dearly loved her husband Connor, she often contemplated whether marrying a military man was the right decision. When they married, he was stationed in the United States, but after a few short years he was selected for a tour of duty in Korea. As she tallied the sacrifices she made to uproot from the Midwest and to follow him across the world on this overseas assignment, she despaired even more. She had left behind family, strong friendships, and a thriving support network and was now displaced in a new location for which she had no affinity. Anger and bitterness were beginning to be her close companions. She absolutely detested almost everything about the country in which she was currently living. The unique smells, foreign food, and difficulties associated with both transportation and communication were weighing heavily on her spirits.

To make matters worse, Connie suffered a miscarriage one year ago. After the loss of her precious baby, Connie felt that she could not go on. When she voiced these sentiments to her physician at their prior duty location, he prescribed antidepressants to help

---

[106] Connie is a purely fictitious character created for the purpose of realistically illustrating the sin and temptation of bitterness and resentment in the military context.

her cope with the grief and loss. However, Connie noticed that after a brief reprieve, her negative and depressed thoughts were coming back with a vengeance, even though she was still on the medication. Her anger, resentment, and sad thoughts seemed to rule her and were negatively affecting her health, outlook, and were even beginning to place a strain on her marriage.

Just yesterday, her husband Connor received orders for a TDY that would cause them to be separated for the next four months. Connie would be even further isolated and alone when he left, stranded amidst a foreign culture, language and surroundings. She could feel the bitter anger rising as she thought of these hard circumstances and desperately wanted relief in some way from the pressure. Although Connie was reconciled to God through Jesus Christ, she was unable to see how that relationship impacted her present trials. In fact, she wondered why things were going so badly for her when she was a faithful Christian. She and Connor typically attended the installation chapel for one of the Protestant services, but despite this, she continued to be thoroughly disturbed by her sad thoughts, anger, and bitterness. Connie knew she needed help, but the type of help she needed and where to seek that help eluded her.

Secular/Psychological Solution to Bitterness and Resentment

If Connie listens to loved ones and close friends for support, they may suggest a number of solutions to her bitterness and resentment. First, it would not be unusual for some well-meaning family members to give the wrong kind of support by encouraging Connie in her bitterness, outrage, and sense of unfairness. They might encourage her to talk and "vent," but not give her the vital truth, perspective, and hope she needs from the Scriptures. Second, they may even convince her that what she really <u>needs</u> is to come back to the states for a time of restoration. While a "furlough" in the U.S. is not necessarily wrong, this type of counsel does not address Connie's heart and will probably add more fuel to the marital fire in her relationship with Connor (especially since finances already prohibited her from going back before).

If Connie were to look to the self-help, popular culture, what type of counsel might she find to overcome her bitterness and resentment? Since her bitterness and resentment contain a type of anger, it would not be unusual for her to find all kinds of counsel on the internet or in magazines that would encourage her to not keep it inside. Depending on the day, she could hear that "blowing up" or "getting it out" might help to clear her mind. American society values women who "stand up for their rights," and it would not be unusual for Connie to find encouragement to speak forcefully to her husband to demand what she wants. Or she might be confronted with counsel that warns against explosive anger because of harmful side effects on the body. In that case, she would be schooled in different ways to manage her anger. This would include everything from "reframing, relaxing and reacting rationally"[107] to utilizing alternative therapies and techniques. Unfortunately, she might even find some Christian writers who advocate being angry with God. Even within some churches, such counsel as, "It is okay to be angry at God! God can take it! Let it all out! He understands your anger and it is okay," has egregiously permeated the thinking and advice of some of the redeemed. While this counsel may be tempting and sound rational, God's Word does not support these claims. A person angry with God is fundamentally accusing God of wrongdoing.[108]

---

[107] Dr. Phil, "Managing Your Anger," http://drphil.com/articles/article/221/ [accessed May 16, 2012].

[108] For a detailed look on this topic that includes a careful look at the Scriptures and that faithfully gives the right way to bring humble, reverent questions before the Lord in times of anguish and suffering, please see the article by Robert D. Jones, "Anger Against God," *The Journal of Biblical Counseling* 14, no.3 [Spring 1996]: 15-20.

The Primary Care Providor

As can be seen above, the types of advice Connie may get from friends, family, and popular self-help arenas could be quite varied, confusing, and even harmful to her spiritually. However, what might Connie find if she were to take her concerns to her Primary Care Physician (PCM) at her present duty location? Since Connie is currently on an antidepressant and experienced a measure of improvement for a season, her doctor's response will probably be centered on helping her to regain a sense of well-being. Because Connie's PCM views her symptoms that resemble depression as primarily an illness, he will more than likely continue to try to fix her body through the use of further medication. In this case, he may recommend that she switch to another antidepressant to test out whether she improves on this new medication. Since there are numerous medications available for the treatment of depression-like symptoms, Connie may go through this process multiple times in dealing with the side-effects of each medication, and seeking to find the therapeutic level or dosage which is the "minimum amount in the body needed to produce the desired response."[109]

The Psychiatrist

Since Connie has no formal diagnosis it is not likely that she would be in contact with a psychiatrist at this point. However, Connie does meet several criteria for Adjustment Disorder with Depressed Mood according to the *Diagnostic and Statistical Manual, Fourth Edition, Text Revision* (DSM-IV-TR). Adjustment disorder (AD) can be defined as

---

[109] Robert D. Smith, M.D., *The Christian Counselor's Medical Desk Reference* (Stanley: Timeless Texts, 2000), 382.

...a stress-related, short-term, nonpsychotic disturbance. Persons with AD are often viewed as disproportionately overwhelmed or overly intense in their responses to given stimuli. These responses manifest as emotional or behavioral reactions to an identifiable stressful event or change in the person's life... The disorder is time-limited, usually beginning within 3 months of the stressful event, and symptoms lessen within 6 months upon removal of the stressor or when new adaptation occurs.[110]

DSM-IV-TR alerts that this disorder could be associated with "suicide attempts, suicide, excessive substance abuse and somatic complaints."[111] It also states that long-term persistence of these symptoms may "signify a progression to other more severe mental disorders."[112] Connie had several "stressors" that predated her slide into anger, bitterness, persistent sorrow and resentment. Even more alarmingly, as stated in the case study above, she is now desperately wanting relief from the pressure she is experiencing. If she continues in this same vein, those who manage her care may recommend other interventions.

The Psychologist/Talk Therapist

Should Connie decide to share her struggles with a psychologist or talk therapist of some kind, what type of counsel might she find? First, a counselor working with Connie would most likely

---

[110] Medscape Reference, "Adjustment Disorders," http://emedicine.medscape.com/article/292759-overview [accessed May 16, 2012].

[111] American Psychiatric Association, *Diagnostic and Statistical Manual of Mental Disorders DSM-IV-TR Fourth Edition (Text Revision)*, (Arlington: American Psychiatric Association, 2000), 68.

[112] Ibid.

affirm the importance of grieving properly over her miscarriage that occurred a year ago. Grief over this loss would be understood, sanctioned and supported. Second, Connie's negative reaction to the country of Korea and its cultures would probably be seen as irrational and pose an opportunity for reframing. One psychologist put it this way:

> There is no objective reason, for instance, why all people in her circumstance would feel similarly as she. Some might find Korea and most of its cultural aspects to be fascinating and well worth exploring, for example. I might explore with Connie the possibility of re-examining her mind-set regarding the cultural differences she is experiencing to see if she might be able to move at least some of (all) the eggs she has placed in her Midwestern-family basket to her "present basket."[113]

Third, Connie's psychologist or talk therapist could be likely to discuss further items that should be explored more deeply by Connie to assist her in the midst of her problems. For instance, the role of her husband, the role of her religious beliefs, and possible environmental change would be topics to explore. Here the therapist would be interested in helping Connie connect with a deeper sense of meaning and even give her the time and space to adapt.

Biblical and Theological Solutions to Bitterness and Resentment

The Bible has much to say about the problems that are plaguing Connie. Below, Connie's bitterness and resentment will be

---

[113] Psychology Practitioner, e-mail communication to author, 8 May 2012.

investigated in the light of the gospel and her union with Christ. Next, three key passages of Scripture will be examined and applied to her circumstances. Finally, a course will be set to assist Connie on her journey of biblical change from a woman of bitterness and resentment to a woman of gratitude, joy, and trust.

How The Gospel and Union with Christ Impact Bitterness and Resentment

What type of impact should the gospel of Jesus Christ have on the bitterness and resentment Connie is exhibiting? The gospel, in all of its beauty is the context in which Connie will want to bathe herself moment by moment. While the truths and applications arising from Jesus' life, death, burial, resurrection, and ascension are numerous, there are two particular facets that will be highlighted here. First, because of the gospel, Connie can know with absolute certainty that she is profoundly loved. God demonstrated His love toward her by sending His Son to die in her place (1 John 4:9-10; John 3:16). Christ willingly laid down His life out of love for and submission to the will of the Father in the greatest act of sacrificial love there will ever be (John 10:11, 15:13). Connie's heart should be thoroughly convinced, strengthened and overjoyed at the love that was and is directed toward her in the cross (Rom. 5:7-8). When Connie is tempted to doubt God's love as a result of her hardships and loss (both past and present), the reality of God's love as displayed in the gospel should silence those doubts with resounding certainty.

Second, because of the crucifixion and resurrection's place in the gospel, Connie can have a transformed perspective on her afflictions and embrace them as an opportunity to be more conformed both to the death and the resurrection of her Savior (Phil. 3:10; 1 Pet. 4:13; Eph. 1:20; Acts 2:24). Galatians 2:20 states that believers are crucified with Christ. While Connie should expect to experience the effects of dying to her fleshly passions and desires on a daily basis (Gal. 5:24), this is not the end of the message of the cross! Christ's resurrection should also speak loudly and joyously to her as well (Eph. 2:6; Col. 2:12).

> These facts surrounding Christ's resurrection stand as proof positive that God will not leave me for dead, but will raise me similarly...Indeed, on the other side of each layer of dying lie experiences of a life with God that are far richer, far higher, and far more intimate than anything I would have otherwise known. In God's economy, death is the way to life. 'Whoever wishes to save his life will lose it,' Jesus says, 'but whoever loses His life for My sake, he shall find it.'[114]

As Connie grasps the reality that her separation from loved ones, her struggle with grief and loss of her beloved baby, the difficulties associated with being in a foreign culture, and the hardships associated with military life are all tools by which God is conforming her more into the death and image of her beloved Savior, her afflictions will take on a different hue of hope and expectation. Just as Christ's death was not the end of the story, her many daily deaths are not the end of her story either! They will lead to a glorious resurrection in which God works in ways far beyond what she can imagine.

How might a better understanding of her union with Christ affect the way Connie deals with her struggles? First, Connie's union with Christ ensures her of an eternal reward in the perfection of heaven. The Spirit placed within her is a deposit guaranteeing her inheritance (Eph. 1:13-14; 2 Cor. 1:22). This spiritual reality should remind her that she will never be fully "satisfied" in this world and all that it can give her. Neither her extended family, a

---

[114] Milton Vincent, *A Gospel Primer for Christians: Learning to See the Glories of God's Love*, (Bemidji: Focus Publishing, 2008), 42.

baby, nor a locale that she loves will fill the ultimate longing that only Christ can fill and that will be fully realized in heaven. Until that day, she will experience a sort of inward "groaning" that eagerly awaits the redemption of her body (Rom. 8:22-25; 2 Cor. 5:2-5). In the meantime, Connie can radically alter how she thinks about her afflictions when they occur by remembering that they are but birth pains compared to the glory that is certain to come. This aspect of her union with Christ should fuel her longing to be with the Lord and her endurance while she remains earthbound in the body.

Second, Connie's union with Christ guarantees that her trials and adversities will be used for both her good and the glory of God. Because Connie is in Christ, she can now relate to God as her Father, and she is part of His family (Rom. 8:15; Gal. 4:6). As such, when hardships occur in her life, she can rest assured that they are being used not as a means of condemnation, but as a means of instruction and correction by her perfect Father (Heb. 12:7; Deut. 8:5). His purpose is to bring about a fruitful harvest in her life that will mature her into greater Christlikeness (Heb. 12:10-11). More about God's use of trials as a form of discipline will be shared in the key passages section of this chapter.

Third, Connie's union with Christ should remind her that she is never, ever alone. Despite her feelings of isolation, the reality is that God is for her, will never leave her, and will never forsake her (Deut. 31:6; Heb. 13:5; Rom. 8:31; Matt. 28:20). As a result of this aspect of her union, Connie can focus less on her feelings of isolation, live in light of the truth, and reach out to others around her with the love of Christ.

Key Passages from Scripture

There are three key passages that will be applied to Connie's problem of bitterness and resentment. First, Hebrews 4:14-16 will be shared to help Connie see the beauty and importance of having Jesus as a faithful High Priest and Mediator. Second, 1 Thessalonians 5:16-18 will be highlighted to help Connie see what God's will is for her in the midst of painful trials. Third, Hebrews 12:5-11 will be examined and applied to help Connie gain a better understanding of how God the Father uses all trials and hardship as a form of loving discipline for the spiritual growth of His children.

The primary audience of the book of Hebrews was Jewish Christians who were experiencing persecution as a result of their identification with Christ and were tempted to "hold on to the symbolic and spiritually powerless rituals and traditions of Judaism."[115] Throughout the book, the "superiority of Jesus Christ" is upheld as opposed to the old covenant of law.[116] With this context in mind, there are three principles that can still be drawn from this passage that will encourage Connie in the midst of her struggles. First, Hebrews 4:14-16 will encourage her with the fact that Jesus is performing the role of *High Priest* on her behalf, interceding at the right hand of the Father day and night (v 14). The love and constant care of her Savior is further demonstrated by His intercession. This should greatly encourage Connie when she feels as if she is alone and isolated or tempted to believe she is forgotten or unloved by God because of her intense trials.

Second, Connie will learn that *Jesus can enter into her sufferings* like no one else can because He experienced the pain, suffering, and separation that life can bring (v 15). He is uniquely qualified to be her mediator, because He too underwent the pain of separation not only from his rightful heavenly home, but also the pain of being separated from God the Father (1 Tim. 2:5; Psalm 22:1; Matt. 27:46; Phil. 4). Not only does He perfectly sympathize with Connie's struggle, He is also uniquely qualified

---

[115] John MacArthur, *The MacArthur Study Bible,* (Nashville: Thomas Nelson, 2006), 1864.

[116] Ibid., 1865. Dr. MacArthur's outline of the book greatly helped me with the context of this passage.

to assist her because He faced all of His sufferings without ever succumbing to sin.

Third, Connie must be reminded of her *responsibility to pray* and approach the throne of grace (v 16). Because she has a faithful High Priest who is interceding on her behalf, can sympathize with her trials and weaknesses, and fully glorified God in the midst of His trials without sin, Connie has the joy and privilege of approaching God in prayer confidently. She must be encouraged to turn to God in the midst of her sadness and separation rather than turning to bitterness and resentment. The scriptures assure her that when she does turn to God confidently in faith, she will find grace and mercy to see her through her time of need.

First Thessalonians 5:16-18 is another key passage that might be used to encourage Connie in the midst of her struggles with bitterness and resentment. The immediate context of this passage has to do with the Apostle Paul giving very practical instruction to the church of Thessalonica on how to live a holy life. Dr. MacArthur comments on 1 Thessalonians 5:16-22 this way: "Paul gave a summary of the Christian's virtues. These verses provide the foundational principles for a sound spiritual life in brief, staccato statements that, in spite of their brevity, give believers the priorities for successful Christian living."[117] With this in mind, Connie can apply these principles to her life in three ways. First, Connie can know that it is God's will for her life *to demonstrate consistent, abiding joy* (v 16). It is likely that Connie is tempted to think that real happiness is a result of her circumstances. However, the Scriptures say the absolute opposite. In fact, throughout the Bible, rejoicing and joy are assumed and commanded (1 Thess. 5:16; Phil. 4:4; Psalm 32:11; 64:10; 97:12). This could not be the case if it had to do with temporal circumstances or the subjective feelings of each individual. Connie needs to know that her joy

---

[117] John MacArthur, *The MacArthur Study Bible*, (Nashville: Thomas Nelson, 2006), 1819.

as a believer is based on the character of God, the Person of Christ, the work that He accomplished on her behalf, and the precious promises that will never fail. Therefore, Connie can know consistent, abiding joy despite her circumstances because her joy does not depend on her location, her being blessed with a child, her physical condition, her earthly husband's presence, her feelings, or her proximity to her relatives.

Second, she should know that it is God's will for her *to be a woman of persistent, constant prayer* (v 17, Eph. 6:18). Connie is utterly unable to effect change in her life. In humble dependence and trust, she will want to take her requests, concerns, praises, and heartaches to the One who alone is able to effect change and give her the strength to carry on. As she draws closer to God in prayer, she will also experience a peace that exceeds all understanding (Phil. 4:4-7).

Third, Connie can know that it is God's will for her *to be a woman of thanksgiving in every situation* (v 18). Gratitude is a potent antidote to bitterness and resentment. Connie's absorption with her disappointments and what she does not have is hindering her from seeing all the ways in which God is blessing her (both eternally and temporally). Just as joy is commanded scripturally, so is constant thanksgiving (1 Thess. 5:18; Eph. 5:20; Col. 3:15,17; Psalm 118:1; 136:1; 1 Chron. 16:34). Connie is promised that as a believer, God is using all her circumstances for good purposes; hence, she always has something to thank Him for even in her darkest hours (Rom. 8:28; James 1:2-4; Heb. 12:11; 1 Pet. 1:6-7; 2 Cor. 1:3-4). By God's grace and the enabling Holy Spirit, as she focuses more on delighting herself in the Lord and thanking Him for all He has done, is doing, and will do, she will find that the root of bitterness in her life is loosening.

Finally, Hebrews 12:5-11 is the third key passage that can be examined and applied in Connie's life to help her see her trials as evidence of her loving Father's involvement and care. This particular passage falls in a section of the book of Hebrews that could be categorized as "the superiority of the believer's privileges."[118] Here, the author of the book turns to discussing not only the importance of persevering in one's faith, but the privilege all believers have of being disciplined by their Heavenly Father.

There are three principles drawn from this passage that should help Connie to persevere and trust God in the midst of her present circumstances. First, based on this passage, Connie should know that *the presence of hardship in her life is a privilege and evidence of her being loved and adopted* into the family of God (Heb. 12:5-8). No doubt, this statement probably seems quite odd and is a major paradigm shift for Connie, but it is nonetheless true. These verses urge her to not despise the Lord's discipline and not to lose heart when reproved by Him. The ESV translation then reminds her, " For the Lord disciplines the one he loves, and chastises every son whom he receives" (Heb. 12:6; Deut 8:5; Psalm 94:12; Prov. 3:11-12; Rev. 3:19). Connie's losses and trials are not proof of a lack of God's love, but a profound evidence of His love and care for her. As an adopted daughter of God, she is receiving the privilege of God's correction and instruction in just the measure that she needs.

Second, *all suffering and trials should be viewed as necessary discipline* given by a loving and perfect Father (Heb. 12:7). More than likely, when Connie reads or hears the word discipline, she thinks of punishment. However, this cannot be the case, especially since the Scripture is quite clear in stating that there is no condemnation for those who are in Christ Jesus (Rom. 8:1). There is no punishment left for Connie since Christ bore all the punishment and wrath of God in her place (Rom. 8:1; 1 Pet. 2:24; Gal. 3:13; Isa. 53:4-6). The word discipline here has to do with instruction, correction, reproof, or training. Discipline comes from the Greek word *paideuo* which can be understood as

---

[118] John MacArthur, *The MacArthur Study Bible*, (Nashville: Thomas Nelson, 2006), 1865.

Originally to bring up a child, educate. Used of activity directed toward the moral and spiritual nurture and training of the child, to influence the will and behavior. To instruct or train...In a religious sense, to discipline in order to educate someone to conform to divine truth.[119]

Just as any loving human parent will instruct, correct, reprove, or train his child, God does the same for His redeemed sons and daughters. To not discipline them would not show love, but would rather be evidence of his hatred (Prov. 13:24, 19:18)! So then, in light of these verses, she should remember that her sufferings are not a result of being punished or condemned by God. Instead, Connie is instructed to view her past and present hardships as a form of loving training from her Father, knowing that He is doing so because of His love for her and His desire for her to conform to divine truth.

Third, although painful, *submission to God's perfect discipline brings great blessing* (Heb. 12:9-11). These verses assure Connie that submitting to God's training and correction will bring sure blessing. Life, shared holiness, righteousness, and peace are some of the good fruit that is listed in these verses that come about as a result of God's discipline. Clearly, this discipline is painful and unpleasant, to say the least (Heb. 12:11), but knowing the sure joyful results of this training far outweighs the temporal pain. Connie will want to emulate her Savior by fixing her eyes on the joy set before her (Heb. 12:2), recognizing her suffering as a proof of God's love and her secured place in the family, and submitting with joy to whatever training He brings, knowing God is going to greatly bless her as a result.

---

[119] Spiros Zodhiates, *The Hebrew-Greek Key Study Bible, New International Version* (Chattanooga: AMG Publishers, 1996), 1657-1658. New Testament lexical aid for the Greek word discipline or *paideuo.*

Bitterness and Resentment and the Process of Change, by God's Grace

How might those who come alongside to assist Connie set about this journey to change? While there are many facets to the process of biblical change, three will be highlighted here to help Connie move from being a woman of bitterness and resentment to being a woman of gratitude, love, and trust. First, in the power of the Holy Spirit and by the strength God provides, Connie will want to *examine, identify, and forsake inferior treasures and broken cisterns.* In Jeremiah 2:13, the Lord declares, "My people have committed two sins: They have forsaken me, the spring of living water, and have dug their own cisterns, broken cisterns that cannot hold water." It is very likely that Connie's bitterness is a result of being denied some of her earthly treasures.

While wanting to be near extended family, having a child, and desiring comfort are not sins in and of themselves, when she elevates them to demands and they are her treasure, she has turned to idolatry (Matt. 6:21; Luke 12:34). When Connie turns away, or forsakes Christ as her ultimate treasure, the search for water begins. This is a fruitless search, however, because Christ is the only source of living water that exists (John 4:10-14, 7:37; Jer. 2:13; Rev. 22:1). In a very real way, Connie is digging cisterns that will not hold water (cisterns of family, location, comfort, wanting children, security, etc). These cisterns and treasures will not quench or satisfy her ferocious thirst and will only enflame her bitterness because they are doomed to fail apart from Christ. Connie will want to forsake all these broken cisterns, turn to her Lord, and quench her thirst in the only One who can satisfy her in this life and in the life to come.

Second, not unlike the two women highlighted in the two previous chapters, Connie will also need to *understand and apply the process of biblical repentance.* This will involve putting off ungodly thoughts, attitudes, speech, and behavior and putting on thoughts, attitudes, speech, and behavior that conform to the

Scriptures. Ephesians 4:31 clearly states that bitterness, wrath, and anger are things that Connie must get rid of (Heb. 12:15 also warns against responding in bitterness to God's discipline). However, the process of biblical change does not end by ceasing bitterness, but by also cultivating an attitude of kindness, forgiveness, gratitude, love and compassion (Eph. 4:32; 5:1-2).

Connie will want to repent of the ways she harbored bitterness against God Himself, her husband, and even the military for the trials she is facing. She will want to repent of the ways she failed to rejoice, pray, and be thankful in the midst of her trials (1 Thess. 5:16-18). She will want to repent of the ways she forsook the Lord and dug broken cisterns, seeking to quench her thirst (Jer. 2:13). Connie will also want to repent of the ways she despised her Father's discipline rather than submitting to Him in trust (Heb. 12:5-11). Connie was surprised by her fiery trials although she was warned not to be and then responded to them with bitterness and resentment (1 Pet. 1:6; 4:12; John 16:33). She will want to confess all of these things to her heavenly Father and rest in the promise that He will cleanse her and enable her to change and walk in a manner worthy of the Lord, filled with thanksgiving, trust, and joy even in the most intense afflictions (1 John 1:9; Phil. 1:6; Col. 1:10, 2:6-7; Psalm 119:71).

The third step in the process of change from bitterness and resentment to gratitude, love, and trust will also require Connie to *become adept at using spiritual tools* God placed at her disposal to overcome this sin and temptation. Although the importance of the people of God as a means of grace was discussed in a previous chapter, it bears repeating again. Those who come alongside Connie will want to remind her that she is part of the family of God (Eph. 2:19). As a daughter of the Most High God, she is part of a bigger family of faith that includes brothers and sisters across the globe (John 1:12-13; Gal. 3:26, 4:6; Rom. 8:15). Connie may be far away from her earthly extended family, but she has the opportunity to build relationships and grow with members of her spiritual family whom she has never met. God will use the members of her eternal family of faith to encourage, rebuke, equip, confront, love, and build her up in the faith to greater maturity (Eph. 4:11-16; Heb. 10:24; 1 Thess. 5:11; Gal. 6:1-2; 1 Pet. 1:22). She is also called to do the same for them with the gifts and talents God gave to her through Christ (Rom. 12:4-8; 1 Cor. 12:12-27). Connie will want to not only "attend" church but also immerse herself in the life of the body of Christ because it is a vital part of her sanctification.

Homework Assignments and Resources on Bitterness and Resentment

Now that we have considered how Connie's union with Christ, the gospel, key biblical passages, and the process of biblical change impact her problems, we want to consider how to integrate these truths into her daily life. Provided below, in no particular order, are thirteen homework assignments that can be used with a woman like Connie in the military context who is battling bitterness and resentment. It is by no means a complete or exhaustive list, but it is a place from which to start. The counselor or friend who comes alongside Connie will want to further alter the assignments by breaking them into smaller segments and giving very specific instructions so that the counselee can be a doer of the Word (James 1:22-25). For instance, a counselor would not want to give his counselee an entire book to read and absorb over the span of one week! Instead, the counselor or friend would break up the book into smaller segments, require certain questions to be answered or thought on, and require a few points to be applied concretely in the counselee's life before the next session.[120] Appendix E also contains an instructional outline that could be used and expanded over several sessions to address the sin and temptation of bitterness and resentment.

---

[120] Please see *Assignment Two* for an expanded example of this concept.

Assignment One

Connie should be greatly encouraged to see examples from Scripture in which God used intense suffering for His glory and for the good of His people. In particular, Genesis 37-50, which details the life of Joseph, and the book of Job would be wonderful places to start. From these Old Testament saints, Connie will see that suffering came about by God's sovereign design toward His beloved children. She will also see that the focus is not on the secondary causes of suffering or catastrophe like Satan, storms, raiders, famine, and malicious people, but on God Himself. The lives of Joseph and Job as recorded in Scripture should cause her to examine whether she is responding to her trials in a way that will honor God. Finally, she should be encouraged to see the amazing ways God used these trials for good in both Joseph and Job's life and trust that He will do the same for her.

Assignment Two

The book, *Be Still My Soul: Embracing God's Purpose & Provision in Suffering* by Nancy Guthrie would be a great resource for Connie. Through the use of 25 classic and contemporary essays, this book considers God's perspective, purpose, and provision in suffering. All the essays would provide her with a better theology of suffering and great encouragement during her trials. However, as a detailed example, Connie could be asked to read the first chapter entitled "Suffering: The Servant of our Joy" by Tim Keller from pages 15-22. She could then be assigned specific questions like these to complete before the next session: #1. Do you agree with the author that our culture is the first to be surprised by suffering? Why or why not? #2. What passages of Scripture from this essay did the author use? #3. Pick out one of these passages and read it every day. Then journal a prayer to God based on this passage. #4. How might God be using your present suffering as a means to your future joy? #5.

Did anything stand out in this reading as new, unique, or troubling to you? If so, why and what was it? #6. How did what you learned in this essay impact your thinking and responses this week?

Assignment Three

The pamphlet entitled *Bitterness: The Root that Pollutes* by Lou Priolo is an outstanding resource that Connie should both read and step through systematically to help her overcome her struggle with bitterness and resentment. This handy resource defines bitterness, helps the reader identify evidences of bitterness in her own life, addresses biblical forgiveness, faithfully discusses how to transform bitter feelings, and equips the reader to make good use of spiritual arsenal to overcome evil. Appendix A of the pamphlet discusses the problem of bitterness at God. This appendix would be highly useful for Connie since her bitterness is a response to the trials that God in His sovereignty is allowing into her life. This section will also help her see the link between her sorrows and bitterness and encourage her to overcome them by God's grace.

Assignment Four

Connie would probably be greatly encouraged by the book entitled *Safe in the Arms of God: Truth from Heaven About the Death of a Child* by John MacArthur. It is very likely that Connie is still sorting through the loss of her baby last year. Any counselor or friend who comes alongside Connie will want to lovingly and patiently assess where she is in this grieving process, and help her to grieve in the truth and in biblically founded hope. This book asks hard questions like, "Where is my child?" "What can we say with certainty to those with empty arms?" "Will I see my child again?" "How shall we minister to those who are grieving?" It then answers those questions and other significant ones scripturally, compassionately and with certain hope.

Assignment Five

Connie typically <u>attends</u> the installation chapel, but she should be given the homework assignment of <u>committing</u> to that gathering or to a biblical church in her area and becoming involved in the body life of that church. Although she is in the Republic of Korea, God has His people everywhere (on the installation on which she lives, as well as the Koreans themselves – interpreters are available in some church locations). Connie has a sense of disconnection and segregation that can be greatly alleviated by immersing herself in the fellowship and life of the local church as God intended. She can thereby mature in her faith and build up and encourage others by the use of her unique gifts for God's glory (Eph. 4:11-16; Heb. 10:25; Rom. 12:5-8). It would also be wise to encourage Connie to seek out a mature Christian woman whom she can meet with one on one in a Titus 2 relationship. This will serve as fellowship, encouragement, and accountability. If she cannot find this "older" woman in her immediate vicinity or church, she may consider using *skype* or *facetime* for this purpose.

Assignment Six

She should read Jerry Bridges' *Trusting God: Even When Life Hurts*, especially chapter twelve, "Growing Through Adversity," to help her see the various ways God may use her hardships away from loved ones in Korea. The resource as a whole will also raise her awareness of God's absolute sovereignty and remind her that God is commanding her destiny for good purposes.

Assignment Seven

Love is a powerful antidote against bitterness and resentment. Connie will want to find numerous practical ways to put the first and second greatest commandments into practice (Matt.

22:37-40). One concrete way to do this would be for Connie to make a list of ways she can serve God and others in her present location. Next, she should pick two of these things and set about doing them. This will enable her to take her eyes off herself and place them on Christ and the needs of others. Another way to show love toward the military members, their families, and the Koreans where she is located is to begin fervently praying for them. Offering up her prayers of petition, thanks, and requests to God (Phil 4:6) on behalf of others will cause her to look beyond herself and to be a vital part of an essential ministry. It will also more than likely encourage an affinity and compassion for the people and location God chose for her (Acts 17:26).

Assignment Eight

Connie will want to do everything biblically possible to strangle bitterness and resentment at their roots. One practical way to do this is by creating a thankfulness list of at least ten to twenty things she is thankful to God for each day. The first five could be concentrated on God's character and attributes. This will help her to see the beauty of God's unchangeable nature in the midst of her ever-changing context, and praise Him for it. Thanking God for both the small and larger details will open her eyes to His kindness that He lavishes on her on a daily basis and keep her focused on all that she does have, rather than on what she does not have. Living a life of thanksgiving directly fulfills the command to be joyful always, pray continually, and to give thanks in all circumstances (1 Thess. 5:16-18).

Assignment Nine

In advance of her husband's upcoming four month TDY, Connie should be encouraged to create a list of goals to accomplish for God's glory, the good of others, and her home while he is gone.

This will practically enable her to seek to be productive during this time rather than wile away her tour in self-pitied absorption. In doing so, she will be fulfilling God's desire for her to be more fruitful and to be known as God's disciple (John 15).

Assignment Ten

Connie would probably be greatly helped in her battle against bitterness and resentment by cultivating a heart for the lost around her. One way to do this would be to task Connie with the assignment of learning more about past and present missionaries to Korea. After studying about historical persons, she could then be encouraged to find current ones (missionaries with Cadence International and/ or Navigators would be a great start as they are often ministering to military personnel and their families at most overseas locations) and talk to them about what they have experienced in the country and their work to make disciples of all nations (Matt. 28:18-20). In doing so, Connie will get the sense that she is blessed with the opportunity of being an "all expenses paid missionary" to whatever location God sends her with the U.S. military.

Assignment Eleven

In accordance with Psalm 119:11, she will want to be proactive at hiding God's Word in her heart through memorization. Passages like Acts 17:26, James 1:2-4, 2 Corinthians 1:8-9, and Jeremiah 17:5-8 speak directly to her struggles. In meditating on these truths, she will be reminded of God's good purposes through trial as well as the importance of making God her sole refuge.

Assignment Twelve

Connie should be given the assignment to reach out and encourage at least one other hurting young woman such as herself. Perhaps she could head up the spouses' welcome section of her husband's squadron, or inquire at the installation's readiness center on how she can assist newcomers, or sign up to check in on new women who come to her church. In any case, she can encourage other women who are missing American "home life" with what she has learned from the Scriptures as well as fulfill God's commands to love others (2 Cor. 1:3-4; Matt. 22:37-40).

Assignment Thirteen

The *Journal of Biblical Counseling* article entitled, "Biblical Help for Overcoming Despondency, Depression" by Wayne Mack is a useful resource for someone like Connie who struggles with crippling sorrow or depression. Within the article, biblical illustrations are given that demonstrate how despondency can be brought about as a result of sinful self-pity, bitterness, and resentment. This is especially instructive for Connie, or anyone who comes alongside her in her battle to overcome these temptations. A study guide to overcoming depression, and several very well thought out homework assignments are also provided at the end of the article.

Conclusion

The women of the military milieu live day-to-day in a unique context. Those who have been redeemed among their number enjoy blessings that go beyond the secular and which can enable them to have hope and joy in the midst of their hardships. These same women encounter tremendous challenges that must be considered by those who come alongside them to counsel, encourage, or equip them if they desire to minister compassionately and effectively.

While the context of women in the military milieu is unique, the sins and temptations they face are not. Rather, these temptations and sins are common to all mankind (1 Cor. 10:13). Hence, the Scriptures and the church of Jesus Christ have lasting solutions to the problems these women face that can never be adequately addressed by the Veteran's Administration, the mental health profession or even the White House. Not only can Christian women in the military milieu cope, but they can thrive. As a result of the gospel, their union with Christ, the indwelling Holy Spirit, and the sufficient Word of God, they lack nothing necessary to wage battles on the spiritual front with precision and triumph (2 Pet. 1:3; 2 Tim. 3:16-17; Psalm 34:9, 84:11; Phil. 4:13).

Those who befriend, counsel, minister to, and love women in the military milieu have a great privilege of being conduits of biblical help and hope. They indirectly support our nation's efforts by equipping women to live well for the glory of God on the home front or on the front lines. More importantly, those who minister to these women can know without a shadow of a doubt that God will multiply their acts of kindness and counsel and thereby reach others through these women wherever they are sent anywhere around the globe.

Appendix A

Survey Result Presentation

Below are screenshots generated from the online survey data that I created by using SurveyMonkey Inc. with their permission[121].

---

[121] SurveyMonkey is not associated with the author, nor does it endorse or sponsor this book. More information can be found at SurveyMonkey Inc, San Mateo California, USA or at www.surveymonkey.com.

How old are you?

		Response Percent	Response Count
18-25 years		7.0%	8
26-35 years		38.6%	44
36-45 years		38.6%	44
46 years or older		15.8%	18
		answered question	114
		skipped question	0

In what capacity are/were you affiliated with the military? Please check all that apply.

		Response Percent	Response Count
I am in the military myself		23.7%	27
I was in the military		25.4%	29
I am the wife of a military member		57.0%	65
I am the wife of a veteran/retired military member		17.5%	20
		answered question	114
		skipped question	0

Christian Women And The Military-Top 5 Temptations

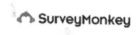 SurveyMonkey

What is/was your military affiliation?

		Response Percent	Response Count
Air Force		75.2%	85
Air Force Reserve		9.7%	11
Army		9.7%	11
Army Guard		0.9%	1
Army Reserve		1.8%	2
Navy		5.3%	6
Marines		3.5%	4
Coast Guard		0.9%	1
		answered question	113
		skipped question	1

Christian Women And The Military-Top 5 Temptations

SurveyMonkey

How long have you been affiliated with the military?

		Response Percent	Response Count
5 years or less		18.6%	21
10 years or less		21.2%	24
15 years or less		24.8%	28
20 years or less		18.6%	21
21 years or more		16.8%	19
		answered question	113
		skipped question	1

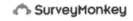
What are the top 5 temptations you have faced while affiliated with the military? Please rank order your selection from 1-5.

	#1	#2	#3	#4	#5	Rating Average	Response Count
Bitterness/Resentment	16.4% (10)	23.0% (14)	27.9% (17)	19.7% (12)	13.1% (8)	2.90	61
Fear	32.8% (20)	18.0% (11)	16.4% (10)	14.8% (9)	18.0% (11)	2.67	61
Pride	37.0% (17)	30.4% (14)	17.4% (8)	8.7% (4)	6.5% (3)	2.17	46
Self-Pity	2.1% (1)	20.8% (10)	25.0% (12)	25.0% (12)	27.1% (13)	3.54	48
Anger	5.4% (2)	16.2% (6)	27.0% (10)	18.9% (7)	32.4% (12)	3.57	37
Emotional/Mental Infidelity	16.7% (4)	4.2% (1)	25.0% (6)	29.2% (7)	25.0% (6)	3.42	24
Lack of Financial Stewardship	0.0% (0)	13.3% (2)	26.7% (4)	40.0% (6)	20.0% (3)	3.67	15
Irresponsibility	0.0% (0)	12.5% (1)	25.0% (2)	37.5% (3)	25.0% (2)	3.75	8
Emotional Eating	17.5% (7)	25.0% (10)	20.0% (8)	7.5% (3)	30.0% (12)	3.08	40
Controlling Attitudes/Behavior	18.6% (11)	27.1% (16)	15.3% (9)	25.4% (15)	13.6% (8)	2.88	59
Withdrawal/Isolation from Others	41.0% (16)	12.8% (5)	10.3% (4)	23.1% (9)	12.8% (5)	2.54	39
Discontentment	25.0% (15)	23.3% (14)	21.7% (13)	15.0% (9)	15.0% (9)	2.72	60
Envy/Jealousy	10.3% (4)	15.4% (6)	15.4% (6)	28.2% (11)	30.8% (12)	3.54	39

Other Temptations (please specify)	16
answered question	112
skipped question	2

Do you have a personal story or situation that you would like to share that will illustrate the circumstances you faced as you grappled with these temptations? If so, please share it below.

	Response Count
	53
answered question	53
skipped question	61

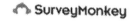
Have you ever sought help in overcoming these temptations from any of the people below?

		Response Percent	Response Count
Chaplain		19.4%	18
Psychologist/Psychiatrist		22.6%	21
Church Pastor		18.3%	17
Supervisor		4.3%	4
Commander		5.4%	5
Ministry Leader		29.0%	27
Friend		82.8%	77
Biblical Counselor		21.5%	20
Other (please specify)			30
	answered question		93
	skipped question		21

Appendix B

Fear Biblical Counseling Outline

I. Finding Comfort in the Character of God
   a. Understanding the Love of God (1 John 4:7-18, 1 Cor. 13:1-8, Ps. 136, Rom. 8:38-39)
   b. Understanding the Wisdom of God (Rom. 11:33-36, Ps. 147:5, Isa. 55:8-9, Jer. 10:12)
   c. Understanding the Sovereignty of God (Ps, 115:3, 139:1-18, Eph. 1:11-12, Dan .4:34-35, Rom. 8:28-29, Isa. 45:7-12)
   d. Understanding the Omniscience and Omnipresence of God (Ps. 139:1-18)

II. Finding Joy and Strength in the Gospel and Union with Christ
   a. Ramifications of Being Set Free (Heb. 2:14-15, 1 John 4:18)
   b. Living Hope, Incorruptible Inheritance (1 Pet. 1:3-4)
   c. Being with the Lord (1 Thess. 4:13-18)
   d. Goal of Faith, Salvation of Soul (1 Pet. 1:9)
   e. No Condemnation (Rom. 8:1)
   f. Recipient of Christ's Righteousness (2 Cor. 5:21, Rom 1:17, 1 Cor. 1:30)
   g. Cleansing in Repentance (Heb. 4:16, 1 John 1:9)
   h. Advocate in Heaven (Rom. 8:27, 34, Heb. 7:25)
   i. All Things for Good (Rom. 8:28-30, James 1:2-4)

j. Spirit of Sonship (Rom. 8:15-17)

III. Battle for the Mind

    a. Learning How to take Thoughts Captive (2 Cor. 10:3-5)

    b. Learning to make Thoughts Obedient to Christ (Phil. 4:4-9)

    c. The obedient victor experiences peace (Isa. 26:3, Col. 3:15, Phil. 4:7, 9, John 16:33)

IV. Learning How to Trust God

    a. Lean not on own understanding (Prov. 3:5-6, Jer. 17:5-10)

    b. Making decisions to trust God (Ps. 56:3-4, 42:11, 28:6-7, Rom. 15:13)

    c. Being thankful always (1 Thess. 5:16-18, Eph. 5:19-20)

V. Distinguishing Between Biblical Fear and Sinful Fear

    a. Fear of the Lord commanded (Deut. 6:13, Ps. 34:9, 1 Pet. 2:17)

    b. Prudent fear that keeps one from danger (Prov. 8:12, 32-36, 22:3)

    c. Sinful fear that springs from a heart of distrust, disbelief, or disobedience (Matt. 10:28, 6:25-34, Phil. 4:6-9, Rom. 5:3-5)

VI. Casting Out Unbiblical Fear

    a. Grow in Love for God (1 John 4:8, Matt. 22:37-40, Rom. 13:8-10)

    b. Grow in Fear of God (Ps. 119:1-2, Deut. 10:12-13, Prov. 2:1-5)

Appendix C

Repentance and Remorse Bible Study

True repentance is characterized by an acknowledgement of sin, a forsaking of wickedness and a turning toward God and his ways. God in his love and holiness will use the Word, the Spirit and the body of believers to prick us and make us aware of our transgressions. Because we as believers have been set free from the law of sin and death, we have the choice to continue in our sin and choose the world's way, which only leads to despair, or allow godly sorrow to lead us to biblical action and sanctification.

It is my prayer that as you carefully, prayerfully and faithfully step through this bible study, that you will gain a greater understanding regarding biblical repentance. Each section has a day-marker by the heading. This study is meant to be completed in 7 days. Please take a moment to ask God to reveal himself to you during this study and to highlight any areas in your life that he desires changed.

I. **What Is Repentance? (Day 1)**

1. What is your personal definition of repentance? Write it out in the spaces below.

2. Take a moment to read through these definitions and summaries on repentance.

   a. The following word is one form of the Greek term used in the bible for repent. "Metanoeo; from meta, denoting change of place or condition, and noeo, to exercise the mind, think, comprehend. To repent, change the mind, relent. Theologically, it means to change one's mind or disposition toward God. More specifically, to repent is to undergo a moral reorientation of the soul in which one acknowledges the error of his ways and turns toward the divinely prescribed way of truth and righteousness."

   b. Jay Adams writes on pages 142-143 of his book entitled, *How To Help People Change*:

   > "There is nothing in the word *metanoia* (repentance) about sorrow; indeed it does not speak of the emotions at all. That is not to say that true repentance will not lead to sorrow, but the word itself carries no such connotation... Repentance is more than regret, even godly regret. Although all true repentance involves regret for having offended God, that emotional side of the process is neither the sum total of repentance nor always manifest to others. In the Scriptures, the evidence of repentance is not regret, but 'fruit' resulting from and appropriate to repentance. That is clear from the preaching of John, Christ, and the apostles."

3. Based on what you just read, how would you redefine your personal definition of repentance?

4. Look up the words penance, guilt, remorse and regret in your dictionary and note their definitions. How is repentance, as defined above, different than these others?
5. Has your life modeled this biblical view of repentance? If not, in what ways has it been different?

II. Scriptural Examples Of The Repentant and/or Remorseful (Day 2-6)

1. *(Day 2)* Please turn to Genesis 4 in your Bible and read the entire chapter.
   a. According to Genesis 4:6-7, what was God's response to Cain's anger? How did God counsel Cain to correct the situation?
   b. Cain chose to murder his brother instead. What was Cain's response after God pronounced his punishment in Genesis 4:13-14?
   c. In your opinion, did Cain display signs of repentance? Why or why not?

2. *(Day 3)* Open your Bible to the book of Exodus and read chapters nine and ten. Study carefully Pharaoh's responses to the plagues brought on him and Egypt by God:
   a. Why was Pharaoh being punished with plagues according to Scripture?
   b. According to these two chapters did Pharaoh ever confess that he was wrong and that he had sinned? If so, why do you think he admitted to such things?
   c. Pharaoh finally let the people go, but later pursued them to the Red Sea (Exodus 13). In your opinion, did Pharaoh ever repent of his deeds and follow God's ways?
   d. Have you ever hardened your heart to God's ways and admitted sin to alleviate the consequences or get rid of guilt?

e. How do you think God would have really wanted you to respond?

3. *(Day 4)* 2 Samuel chapters 11-12 record David's sin with Bathsheba, his pre-meditated murder of her husband, Uriah, and his friend Nathan's rebuke. Please read both chapters now.

   a. What was David's response to Nathan's rebuke in 2 Samuel 12:13? Was his response different than Cain or Pharaoh? If so, how?

   b. After David's son was pronounced dead, what was David's response in 2 Samuel 12:20? Was his response different than Cain or Pharaoh? If so, how?

   c. Read Psalm 51, which was written by David. Who did David say he sinned against in verse 4? According to verses 10 and 16-17, what is God looking for in the life of a believer?

   d. Based on everything you've read, how is it that David was called a man after God's own heart (1 Samuel 13:14, Acts 13:22)? What is applicable to your life as you reflect on the life of David?

4. *(Day 5)* Read Malachi 1-3.

   a. What were some specific reasons God was angry with his people and the priests?

   b. How were the people seeking to appease God? What were they trying to do to cover the guilt of their sins?

   c. What does God tell them to do instead? (Malachi 1:11,14; 2:2, 5-6,15 and 3:3, 9-10)

   d. What do these chapters tell you about what God is looking for when it comes to repentance?

5. (*Day 6*) Please read Matthew 26:31-35, 69-75.
   a. Why do you suppose Peter wept bitterly? Is this evidence of a repentant heart?
   b. According to Acts 4:1-22, how is Peter different? In what ways is this evidence that Peter truly repented?

III. Principles (Day 7)

The following are principles (basic truths or laws) based on Scripture and what we've studied so far. Prayerfully consider each one and ask God for a clear understanding of how to apply them to your life.

1. **The call and need for repentance is universal and applies to all mankind.**
   a. Read Romans 3:23, Acts 17:30 and 2 Peter 3:9
   b. What do these passages reveal about repentance? To whom do they apply?
2. **Repentance is critical for our eternal salvation, but must also be the habitual attitude of a growing believer.**
   a. Read 1 John 1:5-10. How does a believer have fellowship with God and other believers?
   b. What are some characteristics of a growing believer according to 2 Corinthians 3:18 and Galatians 5:22-26?
3. **Repentance is brought about by exposure to and acceptance of God's Word.**
   a. What do Romans 10:13-15 and 2 Timothy 3:16 have to say about the Word of God?
   b. If conviction is brought about by Scripture, what does that practically mean for you as a believer? What might be some consequences of not reading the Word of God?

4. *Repentance goes hand in hand with turning away from former conduct and turning to God and his ways.*
   a. Read Ezekiel 18:30, Acts 3:19 and Acts 20:21. What do these verses say about repentance?
   b. Give a practical example of how you might carry out these commands in your own life.

5. *A true heart of repentance brings first inward and thereby outward change.*
   a. External acts alone will not clear the conscience of an individual. However, true repentance, as accompanied by a changed heart and mind will also take action to please God in faith.
   b. Read Matthew 3:8 and Acts 26:20. What were John the Baptist and Paul preaching?

6. *Repentance is proceeded by freedom and restoration, not slavery.*
   a. What do you think it means to be a "slave to righteousness" (Romans 6:18)? Do you suppose this verse means that holiness is a form of enslavement?
   b. Read Psalm 103:12, Hebrews 10:22, 2 Corinthians 7:10 and Jeremiah 15:19. What do these verses say about our relationship to God and our freedom when we repent?
   c. According to Romans 6:16-23, what does the Bible say about the nature of "slavery" and the wages of sin, versus the wages of righteousness? What really sets us free? A heart of repentance, or a heart of rebellion?

7. *Repentance is tied to the mind and heart, not necessarily the emotions*
   a. Review the definition and summary regarding repentance given earlier in the paper
   b. Are the presence of sad feelings or even acknowledgement of sin enough to satisfy this definition of repentance? Why or why not?

    c.   Read about Judas in Matthew 27:1-5. Was Judas sorry? Was Judas repentant?

8.   ***Repentance has a great chance of being brought to bear through the presence of others in the Body of Christ.***

    a.   The body of believers will often bring Scripture to life. Not only through the teaching of the Word (sermons), but by iron sharpening iron (Proverbs 27:17).

    b.   Often, when people are in the grips of sin they shun fellowship. Being around others who are walking in godliness will bring conviction to the soul who is not. What do Matthew 18:15-17 and Galatians 6:1-3 tell believers to do in regards to sin and church discipline?

    c.   What do all of these verses say about the importance of being in fellowship with other believers in regards to repentance?

Appendix D

Controlling Attitudes/Behavior
Biblical Counseling Outline

I. Finding Comfort in the Character and Attributes of God
   a. Understanding the Love of God (1 John 4:7-18, 1 Cor. 13:1-8, Ps. 136, Rom. 8:38-39)
   b. Understanding the Wisdom of God (Rom, 11:33-36, Ps. 147:5, Isa. 55:8-9, Jer. 10:12)
   c. Understanding the Sovereignty of God (Ps. 115:3, 139:1-18, Eph. 1:11-12, Dan. 4:34-35, Rom. 8:28-29, Isa. 45:7-12)
   d. Understanding the Omniscience and Omnipresence of God (Ps .139:1-18)
II. Finding Joy and Strength in the Gospel and Union with Christ
   a. Rest in Perfect Record and Righteousness of Christ (1 Cor. 1:30, 2 Cor. 5:21, Rom. 1:17; 4:25)
   b. No Punishment and No Condemnation (Rom. 8:1-4)
   c. Joy in God's Perfection and Goodness (2 Sam. 22:31, Deut. 32:4, Prov. 30:5, Ps 18:30, Matt. 19:17)
   d. Jesus Bore Wrath of God on Behalf of Believers (Isa. 53:4-12, 1 John 2:2)
   e. Union and Eternal Love Towards the Saints (John 15:13, Rom. 8:37-39)
   f. Union and Spiritual Fruit (John 15:5,16, Matt. 13:23)

g.   Union and Progressive Christlikeness (Rom. 8:29, 2 Cor. 3:18, Phil. 1:6, Eph. 5:1, Phil. 2:5, 1 Cor. 11:1)

III. God's Sovereignty and Presumptuous Plans

    a.   Planning Without Thought to God Condemned (James 4:13)

    b.   Foreknowledge and Human Length of Days Belong to God Alone (Ps. 39:5, 139:16, 144:4, James 4:14)

    c.   Humble Plans and Submission to God (James 4:15, Matt .6:10, Luke 22:42)

    d.   Presumptuous Planning a Form of Pride (James 4:16)

IV. God's Sovereignty in Daily Life

    a.   In Building (Ps. 127:1)

    b.   In Protecting, Guarding and Watching (Ps. 127:1)

    c.   In Toil, Sleep, and Provision (Ps. 127:2)

V.   Trials as a Means for Good

    a.   Joy Possible in Every Circumstance (James 1:2, 2 Pet. 1:3-4, Rom. 8:28)

    b.   Trials Used for Good (James 4:3-4, Rom. 8:29, John 15:1-2, Heb. 12:7-11)

VI. Journey From Control to Humble, Dependent Planning

    a.   Rejoicing in God's Attributes and Character (Exod. 34:6-7, Num. 14:18, Deut. 4:31, Jer. 9:24, 1 John 4:16, Rev. 1:8)

    b.   Gazing on the Perfections of Christ and Being Transformed (2 Cor. 3:18)

    c.   Repentance for Presumptuous Planning (James 4:13-16, Ps. 127:1-2)

    d.   Repentance for Assuming God's Place (Isa. 46:9, 55:8-11)

    e.   Repentance for Treasuring Earthly Things Above Christ (Matt. 6:19-21)

    f.   Becoming Adept at Humble Prayer, Recognizing God's Sovereignty (1 Thess. 5:17, Rom. 12:12, Phil. 4:6, Eph. 6:18, Matt. 6:10, Luke 22:42, Acts 21:14, Eph. 1:15-23, 3:14-19, Col. 1:9-14, Col 4:2, 1 Thess. 5:16-18)

Appendix E

Bitterness and Resentment Biblical Counseling Outline

I.   Learning A Few of God's (Revealed) Purposes for Hardship
    a. To make us more like Jesus (Rom. 8:28-30)
    b. To cause us to depend more on Him (2 Cor. 1:8-9)
    c. To mature our faith (James 1, Heb. 12)
    d. To cause us to long for our true homecoming (Rev. 21:4)
    e. To make us more fruitful for His glory (John 15)
    f. To prepare us to comfort and encourage others (2 Cor. 1:3-4)
    g. To reveal areas of sin or weakness and discipline us (Heb. 12, Ps. 119:67,71)
    h. To reveal His power, glory, and majesty (John 9:1-3, 11:4)

II. Learning About Jesus as High Priest and Mediator
    a. High Priest and His intercession for believers (Heb. 4:14)
    b. Jesus enters into our sufferings (Heb. 4:15)
    c. The believers responsibility and privilege to pray (Heb. 4:16)

III. Learning About God's Sovereignty
    a. His power, control, and selection of our living locations (Acts 17:26)
    b. His control over every aspect of our lives and days (Ps. 139)

IV. Turning From False Cisterns To The Well of Living Water
   a. 1st and greatest commandment (Matt. 22:37-38)
   b. What it means to have no other "gods" before Him (Exod. 20:3, Deut. 6:14)
   c. Learning how she has placed confidence in "false cisterns" (Jer. 2:13, 17:5-8, 13)
   d. Encouragement to place full trust and confidence in God
V. Learning to Actively Love Others
   a. Turn away from self-absorption and turn to deliberate love and service of others
   b. 2nd greatest commandment (Matt. 22:37-40)
   c. Biblical love defined and described (1 Cor. 13:1-8)

Bibliography

BOOKS

Adams, Jay E. *How to Help People Change: The Four-Step Biblical Process*. Michigan: Zondervan, 1986.

Adsit, Christopher B., Chris Adsit and Marshele Carter Waddell. *When War Comes Home: Christ-Centered Healing for Wives of Combat Veterans*. Newport News: Military Ministry Press, 2008.

Alcorn, Randy. *Heaven*. Carol Stream, Illinois: Tyndale House Publishers, 2004.

American Psychiatric Association. *Diagnostic and Statistical Manual of Mental Disorders DSM- IV-TR Fourth Edition (Text Revision)*. Arlington: American Psychiatric Association, 2000.

Bridges, Jerry. *Respectable Sins: Confronting the Sins We Tolerate*. Colorado Springs: NavPress, 2007.

Carnegie, Dale. *How to Stop Worrying and Start Living: Time-Tested Methods For Conquering Worry*. New York: Pocket Books.

Fitzpatrick, Elyse and Dennis E. Johnson. *Counsel from the Cross: Connecting Broken People to the Love of Christ.* Wheaton: Crossway, 2009.

Fitzpatrick, Elyse and Jessica Thompson. *Give Them Grace: Dazzling Your Kids With the Love of Jesus.* Wheaton, Illinois: Crossway, 2011.

Fitzpatrick, Elyse and Laura Hendrickson, M.D. *Will Medicine Stop the Pain?: Finding God's Healing for Depression, Anxiety & Other Troubling Emotions.* Chicago: Moody Publishers, 2006.

Fortinash, Katherine M. and Patricia A. Holoday Worret. *Psychiatric Mental Health Nursing,* 3rd ed. Saint Louis: Elsevier Mosby, 2004.

Green, Jocelyn. *Faith Deployed: Daily Encouragement for Military Wives.* Chicago: Moody Publishers, 2009.

Grudem, Wayne. *Systematic Theology.* Grand Rapids: Zondervan, 1994.

Hall, Lynn K. *Counseling Military Families: What Mental Health Professionals Need to Know.* New York: Routledge, 2008.

Hallowell, Edward M.D. *Worry: Controlling It and Using It Wisely.* New York: Pantheon Books, 1997.

Henderson, Kristin. *While They're at War: The True Story of American Families on the Homefront.* Boston: Houghton Mifflin Company, 2006.

Horn, Sara. *God Strong: The Military Wife's Spiritual Survival Guide.* Grand Rapids: Zondervan, 2010.

Kay, Ellie. *Heroes at Home: Help and Hope for America's Military Families.* Bloomington: Bethany House Publishers, 2008.

Lewis, C.S. *Mere Christianity.* New York: Simon and Schuster, 1952.

MacArthur, John. *The MacArthur Study Bible.* Nashville: Thomas Nelson, 2006.

MacArthur, John F. and Wayne A. Mack. *Introduction to Biblical Counseling: A Basic Guide to the Principles and Practice of Counseling.* Dallas: Word Publishing, 1994.

Mack, Wayne and Joshua Mack. *Courage: Fighting Fear with Fear.* Phillipsburg: P&R Publishing Company, 2014.

Mack, Wayne A. and David Swavely. *Life in the Father's House: A Member's Guide to the Local Church.* Phillipsburg: P&R Publishing, 1996.

Pink, Arthur W. *The Sovereignty of God.* Grand Rapids: Baker Books, 1930.

Smith, Robert D. M.D. *The Christian Counselor's Medical Desk Reference.* Stanley: Timeless Texts, 2000.

Street, John D. and Janie Street. *The Biblical Counseling Guide for Women.* Eugene: Harvest House Publishers, 2016.

Tripp, David Paul. *Instruments In the Redeemer's Hands: People In Need of Change Helping People In Need of Change.* Phillipsburg: P&R Publishing, 2002.

Vincent, Milton. *A Gospel Primer for Christians: Learning to See the Glories of God's Love.* Bemidji: Focus Publishing, 2008.

Waddell, Marshele. *Hope for the Home Front: God's Timeless Encouragement for Today's Military Wife.* Monument :One Hope Ministry, 2003.

Zodhiates, Spiros. *The Hebrew-Greek Key Study Bible, New International Version.* Chattanooga: AMG Publishers, 1996.

INTERNET DATABASE

Albrecht, Sarah Joy. "God is Awake," http://www.ccef.org/god-awake [accessed April 22, 2012].

Bedell, Zoe Lt., and Marco Werman, PRI's *The World*, "*Female Marine Officer-In-Charge*," http://www.theworld. org/2011/05/female-marine-officer-in-charg/ [accessed January, 2012].

Dawodu, Segun T. "Traumatic Brain Injury (TBI)-Definition, Epidemiology, Pathophysiology," http://www.emedicine. medscape.com/article/326510-overview [accessed January, 2012].

Defense Manpower Data Center Data, Analysis and Programs Division, "Global War on Terrorism Casualty by Reason, 7 Oct, 2001 through 5 Dec, 2011," http://siadapp.dmdc. osd.mil/personnel/CASUALTY/castop.htm [accessed December, 2011].

Department of Defense Military Personnel Statistics, *"Active Duty Military Personnel Strengths by Regional Area and By Country (309A) September 30, 2011,"* http://sladapp.dmdc. osd.mil/personnel/MILITARY/miltop.htm [accessed January 17, 2012]

Dr. Phil. "Managing Your Anger," http://drphil.com/articles/ article/221/ [accessed May 16, 2012].

_____. "Stop Being Controlling and Critical," http://drphil. com/articles/article/93 [accessed April 17, 2012].

Green, Jocelyn. "On the Homefront: Easy Ways to Support Military Wives" http://www.cbn.com/family/familyadvice/ Green_MilitaryFamilies.aspx [accessed May 31, 2012]

Greenberg, William MD. "Medscape Reference: Obsessive-Compulsive Disorder," http://emedicine.medscape.com/ article/1934139-overview [accessed April 22, 2012].

Homeport: U.S. Department of Homeland Security, United States Coast Guard, "Core Values," https://homeport. uscg.mil/mycg/portal/ep/contentView.do?contentTypeid= 2&contentid= 17456&programid=12608&pageTypeid= 16440 [accessed November, 2011].

Joint Education and Doctrine Division, J-7, Joint Staff, "DOD Dictionary of Military Terms," http://www.dtic.mil/ doctrine/dod_dictionary/data/c/3019.html [accessed December, 2011].

Karney, Benjamin, David Loughran and Michael Pollard, *"Comparing Rates of Marriage and Divorce in Civilian, Military, and Veteran Populations,"* http://www.paa2008.

princeton.edu/abstractViewer.aspx?submissionid=81696 [accessed January, 2012].

Ledford, Tranette. "Frontlines and Food Stamps," *Military Spouse Magazine*, http://www.milspouse.com/frontlines-and-food-stamps.aspx [accessed February 8, 2012].

Marine Corps Website, "Core Values: The Values that Define a Marine," http://www.marines.com/main/index/making_marines/culture/traditions/core_values [accessed November, 2011].

Medscape Reference. "Adjustment Disorders," http://emedicine.medscape.com/article/292759- overview [accessed May 16, 2012].

MHN Government Services. "Military and Family Life Consultant Program," https://www.mhngs.com/app/programsandservices/mflc_program.content [accessed April 22, 2012].

National Military Family Association, *"PCS Survey Executive Summary For Moves Between 2008-2010,"* http://www.militaryfamily.org/publications/survey-reports-guides/ [accessed January, 2012].

Official Website of the United States Navy, "Honor, Courage, Commitment," http://www.navy.mil/navydata/navy_legacy_hr.asp?id=193 [accessed November, 2011].

Rational Emotive Behavioral Therapy (REBT) Network. http://www.rebtnetwork.org/whatis.html [accessed April 23, 2012].

Robins, Seth. "Food Stamp Use at Military Commissaries Up Sharply in Four Years," *Stars and Stripes*, http://www.stripes.com/news/food-stamp-use-at-military-commissaries-up-sharply-in-four-years-1.160858 [accessed February 8, 2012].

Secretary of Defense 1996 Annual Defense Report, Appendix G "Personnel Readiness Factors by Race and Gender," http://www.dod.mil/execsec/adr96/appendix_g.html [accessed January 12, 2012].

Shackford, Shane M.S. Ed. " Rational Emotive Behavior Therapy (REBT) and its Application to Suicidal Adolescents," http://www.aaets.org/article101.htm [accessed April 23, 2012].

The White House, "Joining Forces: Taking Action to Serve America's Military Families," http://www.whitehouse.gov/joiningforces [accessed November, 2011].

Uniform Code of Military Justice, "Uniform Code of Military Justice, Congressional Code of Military Law Applicable to all Military Members Worldwide," http://www.au.af.mil/au/awc/awcgate/ucmj.htm [accessed January, 2012].

U.S. Army Website, "Soldier Life: Living the Army Values," http://www.goarmy.com/soldier- life/being-a-soldier/living-the-army-values.html [accessed November, 2011].

U.S. Air Force Website, "Our Values," http://airforce.com/learn-about/our-values/ [accessed November, 2011].

Wallace, Kelly. *"Female Wounded Warriors Thrive Together,"* http://www.cbsnews.com/8301- 500803 162-4195938-500803.html [accessed January 17, 2012].

JOURNALS

Jones, Robert D. "Anger Against God," *The Journal of Biblical Counseling* 14, no.3 (Spring 1996): 15-20.

Selle, Andrew H. "The Bridge Over Troubled Waters: Overcoming Crippling Fear by Faith and Love," *The Journal of Biblical Counseling* 21, no.1 (Fall 2002): 34-40.

ARTICLES

Anderson, Jon R. "Flat Daddies Keep Memories Alive for Fallen Soldier's Family," *Air Force Times*, April 28, 2011.

_____. "Life Size Cutouts Are Keeping Families Connected," *Air Force Times*, April 28, 2011.

Borkovec, Thomas D. "What's the Use of Worrying? A Half-hour of Dedicated Fretting Can Help You Chase Away Insomnia, Indecision and That Uncontrollable Stream of Insidious Thoughts." *Psychology Today*, December 1985.

Luedtke, Heidi. "How the Science of Gratitude Can Change Your Military Life," *Military Spouse*, January, 2012.

Mueller, Patterson Alysia. "iHusband," *Military Spouse*, February, 2012.

Tilghman, Andrew. "Gender Gap Shows in Demographics, Opinions," *Air Force Times*, January 2, 2012.

Printed in the United States
By Bookmasters